Dis-
SATISFIED

Kevin Mullens

Joni
God has not
Did His best in
Your Past.
Never settle for
Less than God
has promised you

FZM Publishing
PO Box 3707
Hickory, NC 28603

ISBN 978-0-692-83250-9

Printed in the United States of America

Table of Content

FOREWORD

The world is obsessed with attempting to be happy. However, I have discovered without the freedom of finances and success, your happiness can only live so long. When you can't pay your bills, and the money coming in doesn't meet the demands of your expenses, happiness is now turned into frustration and worry.

I am confident that when you saw the title of this book the first thing that struck your mind is "What? Dissatisfied? Why should I live a life of being Dissatisfied?" *But the truth is if we don't hate where we are, we will never look for a way out.*

It is the assignment of true leaders to identify, develop, deploy and inspire their followers to stand up, to step forward and to reach toward their maximum potential. Once again, my good friend Kevin Mullens has masterfully written a manuscript that will cause us to propel past our wants and past our comfort zone to reach into the land of the impossible.

In Kevin's newest book, you will be challenged to rethink your strategy and re-adjust your priorities to prepare for life, leadership and success! With a clear path, this book serves as a gold mine for identifying and equipping people to become *"Dissatisfied"* with their present season and stretch to their next season. I have often said that what we do now always determines what we can possess next. If we are going to live on a mission and influence those around us, we have to become dissatisfied enough to make necessary changes in our own lives. By developing, growing and changing we will become the example to help others to grow, change and succeed.

It is my utmost privilege to call Kevin Mullens my friend. Very few people I trust to give them my ear. *"Whoever has your ear, has your future."* Kevin is one of those people I trust. You will not be disappointed in this read.

I personally recommend Kevin's newest book "Dissatisfied." Read it daily... read it more than once... make it your goal to comprehend and digest the words so that they become the very fiber of your success. **"Dissatisfied"** has given me a lot to think about for necessary change and for that I am grateful.

"The Satisfied will always work for the Dissatisfied..."

- Dr. Jerry A. Grillo, Jr.

Dis-SATISFIED

It is essential to know that if you want to move on in life, to succeed, progress and prosper, by understanding the cause-effect relationship between dissatisfaction and motivation you increase the probability of attaining your goals, realizing your dreams and accomplishing greater things in life, beyond your wildest imagination.

Who amongst us has ever considered dissatisfaction as a motivator or even a precursor of success, progress, prosperity and greatness? Any time there is dissatisfaction a desire and the hidden potential for doing and acquiring something more is the affect. Further, any time there is a desire for something more and the potential is unexpressed, ignored or overlooked, dissatisfaction increases and motivation wanes. Without the appropriate levels of dissatisfaction, you will not have the motivation to grow, to do, accomplish or acquire more than what you have or are at any given time. In other words, you will remain stuck in an obscure place and in a never-ending cycle of lack, frustration and failure.

We all have had those moments in our lives when we have experienced an inexplicable emptiness – a gnawing feeling of being discontent. In spite of our accomplishments, our networks and the things we have acquired, that gnawing feeling just would not disappear.

We get up in the morning, put on the appropriate mask to cover this discontentment; the one that tells the world you're OK, but you're not. You're mentally, emotionally and bone achingly tired from the incessant demand from playing the "I'm ok, you're ok" game.

Beyond all our best efforts to make life work, we also long to find the principles that make our life-work matter. Is there a place where our unfiltered voice can be heard and expressed—a place where we manifest our purpose with unquestionable clarity? We all long for a meaningful place in the world to *belong* to—a community of like-minded people who are on a similar path. We crave for a community that embraces us without condition, doubt, and struggle. We aspire to be seen and appreciated for who we really are and to find that authentic place of truth. It is only when we find that place that we at last will be relieved of our dissatisfaction.

Kevin Mullens knows exactly where that place is and how to get you there. He has postured himself to be your literary tour-guide. It is from this place that vulnerabilities are changed into vivid displays of authenticity. It is from this place that we gain the courage and conviction to pursue our dreams, maximize our potential as wealth creators, difference makers and agents of change within our spheres of influence.

It is in the pages of this book that the secret for living a meaningful and fulfilled life is revealed. Living a meaningful and fulfilled life starts in a strange place called dissatisfaction.

This book is a page-turner. Read it then share it. You will be glad you did.

- Dr. Cindy Trimm, Best Selling Author and Life Strategist

PROLOGUE

If life has been really good, TODAY can be GOODER; in a new and exciting way. If life has been very difficult or a consistent struggle, TODAY, you can move beyond the difficulties into a more rewarding and fulfilling experience. One not absent of adversity, but one where you walk in longer seasons of victory, peace, joy and favor.

Whatever may have been before, TODAY is different. And you can choose, right now, to make it different in a good way. It starts with your thought life. Your thoughts determine your reality, and TODAY you will choose to think more positive and make better decisions. Your future isn't determined by your past but by your expectations! Whatever you expect in life is what you'll get. If you expect to be a victim, that's what you'll end up being.

Today, you can set those expectations at the highest level that you can imagine. TODAY is different, and TODAY you can do much, much better. It's time to move away from procrastination and self-imposed limitations and demand better from yourself.

TODAY is filled with great challenges and with even greater promise. Make the decision to step up to the challenge and to fulfill the highest promise of this day. Tomorrow is influenced by TODAY. TODAY is different, and is yours to live with purpose, discipline, focus, enthusiasm and passion. Start TODAY! Set higher standards TODAY! Live life to its fullest TODAY! For TODAY is the day the Lord has made, and we will rejoice and be all that we have been called to be!

Kevin Mullens

CHAPTER ONE

POTENTIAL!
It's Not Where You've Been… It's Where You're Going

You are full of potential. If you knew what you are really capable of, you would probably struggle to believe it. When you perform and live beneath your potential you limit the supernatural gifts you were born with from developing.

Ordinary is something you are taught. You may have been infected with the idea that you are not to stand out and that it is ungodly and selfish to pursue and desire more. The people you were raised around likely shared a set of common goals and beliefs like go to school, get an education, get a good job, work towards retirement and play it safe. Even the people who love you are guilty of telling you that reaching higher and pushing limits will probably get you hurt and leave you constantly disappointed

You weren't put here to just survive...You were put here to make a difference and to thrive.

You're here to reach your full potential and to live abundantly as promised by God. If you aren't growing, then you are wasting your potential and risk being judged as an unprofitable servant. It's okay to be pleased with your results, but it isn't okay to be satisfied. No matter how well you are doing, you have more potential in front of you than the potential you've developed in the past. When you have reached any accomplishment, it's not a time to relax but to press on—become more, do more, serve more and earn more. When you stop striving to be more, do more, have more and contribute more, then you are settling for something less than what you are truly capable of.

The full inventory of heaven is within you so do not die with unused talents hidden away. Choose to develop your skills and become a vessel in which God can flow through freely. As for me, I am never satisfied; less of me and more of God.

WHAT IS STOPPING YOU?

I believe fear is the main reason most people do not unleash their full potential. Maybe you are afraid of other people judging you. If you share your voice, people will hear you, and you can't control what they think or say. You doubt yourself, so you withhold your gift instead of boldly sharing it. You might be afraid of failure. Failure is just part of success, but maybe you believe that failure would define you; that it would be an identity and not simply an event.

As crazy as it is to believe, you might avoid living up to your full potential because you fear success. Your success might require responsibilities you are not comfortable with, or maybe you are worried you would leave people behind.

Perhaps you are not taking the massive action necessary to reach your full potential because you think you have time. You do not do what you should be doing today, telling yourself you will always have tomorrow. So many lose out on experiencing a remarkable life because they live in a state of "Tomorrow."

There's a saying that your business is a direct reflection of WHO you are – if it's not growing, you're probably not growing. If that's true for you, perhaps now is the time to take a risk? The breakthrough you seek is impossible without confronting the things that currently hold you back. There will never be victory without a battle. This battle of course is more internal, and the inner critic will sabotage your every move if you don't silence it by taking the necessary risk to grow.

This doesn't mean jumping out of a moving train, throwing your life savings in the stock market, or swimming with sharks. I know with absolute certainty that your ability to create what you truly want in your business is your willingness to take risk. The people who accomplish great things in life are risk-takers. If you look at history, it is filled with leaders who had the courage to "push the limits" and take risks—like pursuing insane ideas or expressing radical, unpopular opinions that were met with resistance. Today, we reap the benefits because of these brave people—trailblazers who were willing to take risks that transformed our world for the better. It's the key to unlocking your true potential!

Without risk, you're doomed to stay in the same place, as the same kind of person, creating the same results. What's the most immediate benefit you'll experience by pushing yourself?

You get to find out WHO you really are and experience your untapped talent and potential like never before. There's a quote I know you have heard... *"Our deepest fear is not that we're inadequate. Our deepest fear is that we're powerful beyond measure."*[i] So let me ask you—do you know WHO you, or more importantly, WHOSE you are? Are you tapping into your real talents or just constantly settling?

Bottom line... are you risking enough? Risking ordinary for extraordinary.

"God's gift to us: potential. Our gift to God: developing it." - Author Unknown

Is what you are doing right now helping you to produce the results you need in the future? Be honest! Is there something else that you could be, or should be doing to produce the future results you need in order to manifest your God Dream?

You must pay for the future results you desire by paying the price now. If what you are doing right now isn't helping you to deliver the future results you need, then you are stealing from your future. At some point, your future will arrive and greet you with the disappointment of not having done what needed to be done earlier. Ten years from now will not be any different if you do not change your course and do what is required to produce a favorable future.

You pay for your future results with the actions you are taking "NOW." You rob from your future when you don't. The time you spend taking calculated risk and developing your skillset is a down payment on your future results. The future always arrives faster than you expect. Your future is unfolding through today's decisions so DECIDE to NEVER SETTLE.

Decide to stop robbing your future through complacency and inactivity.

Potential is in the acorn; it is potentially an oak tree. Your potential lies in your ability to learn, train, overcome adversity, prepare and believe. When we are honest with ourselves, we know that we can be more, do more, serve more, create more, have more, and make a far greater contribution than we are now. You were given this life for a purpose. What you need is already inside of you; develop it. Own your space. Build your personal equity. You are here for a reason. Face your fears, and become the very best version of yourself.

Kevin Mullens

CHAPTER TWO

SETTLERS!
Are Always Satisfied With Status Quo

CONTENTMENT VERSUS SATISFIED

Content means that you have the ability to be happy in the life you're living; you have the ability to be grateful for what you have and enjoy life. I'm very content, but I'll never be satisfied!

I believe that if you ever feel completely satisfied with everything in your life, you haven't set the bar high enough. To say that you're satisfied with everything in your life is just a way to justify giving up on your dreams. You have given into the temptation to accept mediocrity. You have settled for being good rather than striving to be great. I encourage you to not allow yourself to be completely satisfied with your life. The only time you should allow yourself to stop striving to be better is when you're six feet under.

What if Rosa Parks had been satisfied with sitting in the back of the bus? What if scientists, explorers and medical experts became satisfied with their research?

Do not settle down where you are but rather keep pushing boundaries previously thought impossible and discover your limitless potential. Wherever you are now fails in comparison to where you're capable of going.

"Settling for what is comfortable is one of the biggest enemies to our enlargement...In every season of life...we need to be committed to enlarging our personal capacity (even when it's not comfortable). We need to refuse to be satisfied with our latest accomplishments, as what we've accomplished is no longer our potential because it has been realized." - Christine Caine

THE MINDSET OF A "SETTLER"

The available becomes the desirable. The desire is available if you continue to pursue. Those who settle live in a prison of being okay at where they are. They never look to see if they can have more, do more or be more.

I am not attempting to destroy the importance of being content when I say do not settle or use the word dissatisfied. There's a difference between contentment with what God is doing and being dissatisfied at where you are. I'm telling you right now you will never succeed if you are not dissatisfied at your present situation or season.

"Until you hate where you are, you will never look for the door out of where you are." - Dr. Jerry Grillo

CONSTRUCTIVE DISSATISFACTION

- *Dissatisfaction doesn't get the respect it deserves.*
- *Dissatisfaction is a good thing.*

Constructive Dissatisfaction is what leads to growth when utilized as purpose driven motivation. It propels us beyond **complacency** into **excellence.**

- *If you are satisfied with the status quo, then you are not growing.*
- *If you are satisfied with your current position or income then you have surrendered your future by settling.*

Growth comes from believing that things can be better. This doesn't mean you cannot be content or happy. What it does mean is that you have discovered something about you.

1. **You Are Worth More!**
2. **You Deserve More!**

Never apologize for being dissatisfied, as the supernatural within you is always growing, expanding and hungry for more.

Many confuse being dissatisfied with being dishonorable. My dissatisfaction doesn't make me hate what I have got in life. On the contrary, it states that I love what I have, and I want more. I want to be more, do more and help more. Dissatisfaction is the voice of my intended destiny shouting, *"DON'T SETTLE! Don't stop reaching and growing! Don't get complacent!"*

There should be an ambitious drive in us to produce and

perform at the highest level possible whether it is spiritual or natural.

You are ready to grow when you are so dissatisfied with the way things are that you can no longer accept them. It is then that you qualify for the best things in life. You are dissatisfied with what you are because you know that you can be more. You are dissatisfied with what you are doing because you know that you can do more. You are dissatisfied because you know that you can have more, and when you do more, become more and serve more, you earn more.

Dissatisfaction is what gets us unstuck and moving in the right direction. Dissatisfaction compels you to TAKE ACTION. Dissatisfaction is the root of your breakthroughs.

Complacency is a killer, and it is our worst enemy. When your expectations and standards are lowered, then complacency sets in.

Constructive dissatisfaction kills complacency and helps maximize your talents.

Dissatisfaction is a key to success.

Decide to do the things necessary every day to move away from the season of struggle. ***Enough is enough!*** It is only through your day-to-day commitment that your special God given greatness within you flows outward.

A breakthrough requires that you finally decide that your current results are no longer good enough. Yes, you must be honest with yourself. Sometimes you have to reach a *"THRESHOLD,"* that place where you can't—or won't—

allow things to continue the way they are now. You will no longer tolerate where you are.

A threshold is the UNWILLINGNESS to accept things as they are any longer.

You must start by abandoning *Self-Limiting Beliefs*. The results you are producing now are the results of your belief system. You have been infected with your beliefs for a long time, as you are the product of previous thinking. Do not ever abandon your dream but abandon all negative mindset and beliefs. Adopt a new empowering mindset. The proof that you have abandoned a limiting belief and adopted a more empowering one will be visible in your **ACTIONS**. New beliefs will cause you to take new actions that produce new and better outcomes, but you must understand that just saying the words about your new beliefs won't change anything. You have to change what you are doing (habits), or the belief has not taken root in your life.

Breakthroughs are the result of massive, consistent actions taken over time. Getting yourself to take massive action is a small breakthrough on your way to greater breakthroughs. Every step inches you closer. Every trial, every mountain contains a lesson. Rewards are just on the other side of adversity. The process is maturing you and qualifying you for the next level of living. You are now the architect of your destiny.

Stop thinking small and stop limiting the supernatural hand of God from creating in you an abundant life of INCREASE and FAVOR. If God is your Father then you have access to an unlimited SOURCE. Have you discovered all that is available to you?

Ask for BIG things! Whatever you are currently thinking...**THINK BIGGER**! Your attitude in every moment defines what you are seeking. What you seek is what you get.

"Ask me, and I will make the nations your inheritance, the ends of the earth your possession." Psalm 2:8 NIV

"And ALL things, whatsoever you shall ask in prayer, BELIEVING, ye shall receive." Matthew 21:22

"Therefore I say to you, whatever things you ask when you pray, believe that you receive *them*, and you will have *them*." Mark 11:24

"How many believes you can't ask God anything without receiving. Ask and you shall receive. He said, "You have not because you ask not. You ask not because you believe not. Ask and you shall receive. "ASK ABUNDANCE" that your joys may be full." God wants to pour out His blessings." - Prophet William Branham

To be average is to settle for a life determined by others. The opposite of greatness is not failure; the opposite of greatness is **mediocrity**. Some have mistaken average for being humble or content, but it is not. It is failing to recognize that God created you in His image, and He requires INCREASE out of you. Jesus told the disciples that they glorify the Father when they bare much fruit (John 15:8). To have an average mentality is to resign yourself to a life of unreached potential. You are capable of achieving whatever you focus on and truly desire. What would your life look like if it looked exactly the way you wish? Take control, take the initiative, and you can make it so.

An average mindset is the most destructive type of mentality to have because it is fully accepted by our culture. No one will ever challenge you to expand your perspective and break out of that mediocre state of mind. *The status quo is popular because it requires no skill or discipline.*

Pulling away from dream stealers and deciding to live up to your full potential will create distance from you and those who live in survival mode; accepting whatever comes their way. The state of your vision or mindset will determine your level of activity, expectation and what you will be able to accomplish. Remember, that you are destined to be whatever you DECIDE to be. Let others live a small life, but not you. Let others settle for the path of least resistance, but not you. Go relentlessly; pursue the life God promised you.

"Don't let the opinions of the average man sway you. Dream, and he thinks you're crazy. Succeed, and he thinks you're lucky. Acquire wealth, and he thinks you're greedy. Pay no attention. He simply doesn't understand." - Robert G. Allen

Real, meaningful success is a matter of expressing on the outside some of the unique and abundant value that's on the inside. Every great achievement begins as a vision, guided by purpose and ends as a real, tangible substance. Whatever you truly desire, you already have within you. Fulfilling that desire is a process of bringing it to life in the world around you. Take the vision that is inside and show the rest of the world how it looks and what it can do. Do what is necessary to manifest the inner vision that only you can see into outer value that everyone can find useful and inspiring. Dive deeply into the rich abundance that lives within you. Feel the power of your dreams that long to be expressed, and let that imagery flow out through your actions.

Your greatest achievements are already yours. Act on them and let the whole world experience their value too. The world is waiting on you! Don't wait for someday.

- *This is the day.*
- *This is the moment.*
- *This is your opportunity to live.*
- *Live life unlimited*!

Let go of any thoughts of unworthiness or limitation. You absolutely deserve every joy you can imagine, and you're fully capable of creating them all.

Your future starts NOW!

"Now the children of Reuben and the children of Gad had a very great multitude of cattle: and when they saw the land of Jazer, and the land of Gilead, that, behold, the place was a place for cattle; The children of Gad and the children of Reuben came and spake unto Moses, and to Eleazar the priest, and unto the princes of the congregation, saying, Ataroth, and Dibon, and Jazer, and Nimrah, and Heshbon, and Elealeh, and Shebam, and Nebo, and Beon, Even the country which the LORD smote before the congregation of Israel, is a land for cattle, and thy servants have cattle: Wherefore, said they, if we have found grace in thy sight, let this land be given unto thy servants for a possession, and bring us not over Jordan." Numbers 32:1-5

Moses Reproves Reuben and Gad

"And Moses said unto the children of Gad and to the children of Reuben, Shall your brethren go to war, and shall ye sit here? And wherefore discourage ye the heart of the

children of Israel from going over into the land which the LORD hath given them? " Numbers 32:6-7

The children of Reuben and Gad passed through the wilderness experience and were at the doorway to living in the Promised Land. They had lost all inspiration to fight one more battle. They instead SETTLED!!! They literally asked Moses to just let them stay in the land of Jazer as it would be good for their cattle. They were willing to forego abundance and prosperity. They willingly surrendered their divine right to live in a land flowing with wealth because they became satisfied. Their decision to not cross Jordan which meant death; cast a shadow of defeat within the camp and they discouraged the hearts of their brothers and sisters. *"Shall they go to war and you just sit here?"* I can feel the anger rising in their fearless leader.

We live so selfish sometimes that we don't realize the very battles we are running from are the very things appointed by God. Your willingness to face the mountains standing in your way give your friends, family and colleagues hope that if you can conquer the mountain maybe they can to.

So many people quit three feet from gold. I wonder how many others looking to us for strength and guidance have become satisfied with crumbs when a feast fit for kings was just on the other side of the mountain. Do not run from the mountain. Faith runs towards the mountain because faith knows the rewards in which you seek are just on the other side. Don't you dare quit on God, and don't quit on your dreams and discourage those that are connected to you. Don't convince yourself that where you are is okay. Your life provides a GPS for others that it might guide them to the richness life has to offer.

So many people are in the valley of decision waiting on deliverance. Answer the call; like Isaiah said, *"Here am I; Send me"* (Isaiah 6:8). Make a decision today to "CROSS OVER."

"Speak to the Israelites and say to them: 'When you cross the Jordan into Canaan." Numbers 33:51 NIV

We are at the river and the Promised Land is in sight. The voice of settling makes a great argument on why staying put is safe. How much longer will you be pushed aside by your circumstances? Are you influenced by the world or the Word? Today we are "Crossing Over." We will cross over into that Promised Land of Abundance—from the impossible to possible. This is a time of unstoppable increase and uncommon favor. From scarcity and defeat to prosperity and victory. What God has started in us, He will surely complete. No more waiting. No more delays. It is time to CROSS OVER and take ownership of what was promised through unwavering faith.

CHAPTER THREE

HUNGER!
Is Never Satisfied

How hungry are you for the life you have envisioned? Every day you have to be HUNGRY! I often think of that amazing speech by the great Les Brown, "You gotta be HUNGRY."

Dissatisfied people are always hungry. They are ambitious, driven and they're self-motivated. Not only are dissatisfied people tirelessly working, but they're also working with a tremendous sense of urgency.

They are hungry to be more. They know in order to earn more they must become more. They are dissatisfied because they recognize that their potential is far greater than what they have accomplished to date. They do not live on previous victories. They will outwork anyone and everyone around them. They start earlier, stay later and do more in the hours in between. This has always been my personal secret to success.

YOU CAN BE HUNGRY TOO.

(27)

Leaders who are dissatisfied love working; they love producing and winning. They don't have any trouble finding the motivation to get out of bed in the morning. They live life with the expectation that they can dream big, work hard and enjoy the life they desire. You never hear a leader say, *"Don't work too hard,"* or *"Take it easy."* It's unlikely that you are actually working too hard, and if you are habitually taking things easy; then neither of these serves you very well.

Unmotivated and complacent people don't love working hard and paying the price. Work is simply a means to an end to them, and that end is their survival. They spend their life working for the weekend and approach business opportunities with the same mindset. You hear non-producers say things like, *"Back to the grind."* They use that word in a way that is one hundred eighty degrees opposite the way the entrepreneur uses it.

The grind is good because it's what manifests your desires. The good news is you don't HAVE TO do this; you GET TO do this! The millionaire mindset is manifested by applying the millionaire's GRINDSET. Less posting about what you plan to do on social media and more doing what you know needs to be done.

EARNING VERSUS DESERVING

Here's something that probably sounds like your grandmother, but you know it's the truth. *"No one owes you anything."* Not your parents. Not your government. Not your school system. Not your church. Not your company. You become a victim and surrender your personal power to make a difference when you live in this mindset.

This sense of entitlement is disabling. It disempowers you and infects the mind, and it will convince you to rationalize the reasons you don't have what you want. Those that take full responsibility for their actions are able to guarantee the outcomes they desire and can live knowing they are in control!

Entrepreneurs don't live life with an attitude of entitlement. They know that no one owes them anything. They understand the difference between thinking you deserve something versus earning something. They believe they can have anything they want by doing the work necessary.

The *"all talk, no action"* people always feel a sense of entitlement and are always living as if they are owed something. This of course leads to a life of excuses and complaining.

"The dream is free. The hustle is sold separately." - *Unknown*

Hustle is not a mere cliché that's thrown around by entrepreneurs. If people are telling you that you are always working; you're probably on the right track.

It's very popular to say "work smarter, not harder," but these ideas are not mutually exclusive. If you're going to succeed on a massive scale, if you're going to hustle, you are going to need to work smart, and you are also going to need to work hard with an ALL IN mentality. There is nothing about the word "hustle" that suggests a way to succeed that doesn't require hard consistent work. The definition of "hustle" has hard work built-in. Most don't want to work with a sense of urgency. To me, the word "hustle" means to work with a great sense of urgency. When? NOW! It means to move quickly, to get things done and to produce bigger results faster.

Each one of us is trying to make up for some amount of lost time and that is the purpose of hustle—the pursuit of reaching your personal summit. It's about doing "whatever it takes" and pursuing opportunity with unusual determination and great urgency; like your life depends on it, because it really does.

When you have a vision without action, or hustle, it is just a wish. Action without vision is a nightmare. You need both vision and hustle to achieve great things. One is incomplete without the other. Your vision guides you, and your hustle propels you. Unfortunately, most people settle for the dream because it doesn't cost them anything and it's easier. Having a dream requires no price to be paid. Don't just be a dreamer; be hustling in targeted and critical areas such as your mindset, spiritual life, connections, skill development, appointments, trainings and any productive activity that will materialize your vision. You will pull your desired goals to you at a quicker pace through HUSTLE.

HUSTLE IS ACTION ON STEROIDS!

You can always tell a hustler because it looks like they're working as if they're running out of time. Their motor is always running at a higher pace than everyone else. The hustler is constantly in motion.

Hustlers don't procrastinate. They do what they need to do now. No one has to ask them or remind them what they're supposed to be doing. Instead of sitting around like they have more time than work, they work like they have no time at all.

Most people do things when it is convenient, and they don't want to work consistently. Hustlers hustle 24/7/365. They work until they reach their goals, and then they choose another goal to complete. They don't spend time distracted. They remain focused at the task they need to do in order to get what they want. Hustlers don't hustle when they feel like it or every once in a while. They hustle, and often double up on the hustle in order to accelerate the process of seeing their dreams come true at a faster pace!

You can't fake the hustle. Don't be a "wannabe" diamond. It doesn't cost you anything to think like a diamond; but will you work like a diamond? Will you endure the pressure and stay the course to shine bright like a diamond? Commit wholeheartedly to putting in the effort that will position you in the center of your desired destiny.

"H.U.S.T.L.E."

- Honestly
- Utilizing
- Scripture
- To
- Live
- Entrepreneurially

The hustler knows that success is no accident. They know that living *"Life Unlimited"* isn't going to happen by accident. So the hustler very intentionally designs the life that they want for themselves. They ignite their intention with purposeful actions.

Hustlers are internally driven to do more. Intentionality is a mindset. The hustler relentlessly pursues the exact life that they want. Luck/Favor loves a hustler, but only because the hustler is always pursuing the things that they envision. Hustlers hustle by intention. They actually apply Kingdom principles and leave nothing to chance.

Ask the hustler why they focus on wealth creation, and you will discover that what they seek isn't the ability to buy "things." The hustler seeks freedom above all else; the ability to live without financial worries. Financial freedom provides choices and options. To contribute more, to tithe more and to give more!

To a hustler, a lack of anything they need or desire is simply fuel that drives them to hustle harder.

Top producers embrace tough, hard work. Uninspired people resent the process altogether. If you are going to be successful, you are going to have to love doing the necessary work. You almost have to be uncomfortable when you are not doing the work, as it has become a part of your DNA.

"Ambition" is the motivating factor behind "hustle" and sadly that can't be taught. You either have that or you don't! The bad news is, there is no faking hunger. You either want success really bad or you don't. It's that simple, but once you're hungry enough, doing whatever it takes will come naturally. A way of life! So if you will commit to an *UNRELENTING PURSUIT* of your goals, your God Dream will materialize and bring you fulfillment and purpose.

If you love getting your hands dirty, getting in the trenches and doing the things daily most unsuccessful people avoid; then welcome to a remarkable life of success.

Success is the result of designing the life you want for yourself and taking massive action to bring that vision to life. Great things come to those who TAKE ACTION!

You are ordained for success and significance. The seeds of greatness are within you.

"The will to win, the desire to succeed, the urge to reach your full potential...These are the keys that will unlock the door to personal excellence." - Confucius

Kevin Mullens

CHAPTER FOUR

GREATNESS!
The Enemy Of Average

Take something ordinary and add focus, commitment and relentless effort, and you will have greatness.

Greatness arises out of the common and the ordinary.

The raw material of greatness is not that special. A magnificent mansion is made out of ordinary wood, bricks, mortar and nails. A literary masterpiece is printed on ordinary paper. A beautiful symphony is performed with ordinary musical instruments. God doesn't take great things and make them greater. He takes ordinary things and touches them and that makes them greater.

Greatness depends not on what we have to work with, but on *"what we do with it."* Greatness is achieved not because of what we have but as a result of what we do. You don't have to have the best to be the best. Take what you have and decide right now to do your best with it, and you will achieve greatness in the end.

Greatness by definition can be explained many different ways, yet it is within the reach of anyone. Understand that greatness comes from common, ordinary beginnings. Whoever you are, wherever you are, whatever you have to work with, greatness is always waiting for you to make it happen.

"You have given me your shield of victory. Your right hand supports me; YOUR HELP has made me GREAT." Psalms 18:35 NLT

Success is attached to those who become unrelenting in their pursuit. ***Unrelenting!*** It isn't the action that gets you results. It's the consistent action that produces results. Relentless, nonstop, unusually determined, tenacious action!

Most will commit to taking action once or twice. It's the taking of that action over and over again, time after time, relentlessly without wavering that guarantees success. The action may not even be right at times, but over time, it gets you closer and closer to the place you intend to arrive at.

The most important step is the first step. The hardest step to success will be your first step. It's important to take that first step. Getting started is always the hardest, but no one talks about the second step, or the third and the ten thousandth step. The relentless action from that first step is what moves you forward—little by little, moving closer and closer. ***Being unrelenting is difficult.*** You reach many plateaus; your progress stalls and may even go backwards. But being unrelenting means learning to live within the struggle and temporary setbacks, continuing on even when it feels like no progress is being made. Some will wonder how you go on, why you aren't frustrated, disappointed, or haven't quit. They don't understand that you can't stop but must continue; that it's *"what you do"* because it's *"who you are."*

"Criticism is the death gargle of Non-Achievers."

Most will criticize you for plowing on and call you stubborn. They'll suggest that you don't know when to quit and try to darken the light of your dream; but a small few will find inspiration in how you continue. They'll begin to understand that it isn't a single action that has made you successful, but the consistent unrelenting pursuit, day after day without faltering, that makes the difference. This is your secret! This is why you shine bright like a diamond. It's pushing past the pressure that forces the coal to become the diamond.

Winners know that "sometimes" isn't a strategy. Successful people do daily what unsuccessful people do occasionally. There are seven days in a week; not one of those days is named "someday." People that win consistently focus on taking consistent action. Losers are rarely consistent and quit often; they do some things that need to be done but only some of the time.

Any single action they take alone isn't what allows them to succeed. It's the "consistency of action" over long periods at a sustained pace of time that builds success. Their momentum isn't waiting on luck, but through hard consistent work they know they will create their own luck.

Winners pay the price in advance for their success.

You will have to be inconvenienced in your life to do something remarkable and meaningful. Balance is very important but being unbalanced for a season is also important. **Become temporarily unbalanced** at work when it's inconvenient.

I hope you're mature enough to understand that I am in no way advocating ignoring your family. I am simply showing you that you must be unbalanced at times to become successful.

To get temporarily **UNBALANCED** means you sacrifice life's little luxuries—like time with friends, events, and definitely sleep. It's inconvenient and hard, but that's the point. You have got a burning desire and a hunger, as well as an unusual determination to live life on your terms.

Winners Pay the Price…Whatever is it! The price might be countless hours of hard work with little sleep, grinding it out twenty-four seven. That price might be giving up a lot of hours of things that bring them pleasure, like hanging out with friends or watching hours of sports on television. Winners know that the investment of time comes before they can generate results; they understand the pursuit of something and the intensity in which they pursue it is what qualifies them for remarkable results.

Most people, on the other hand, expect a handout. They believe that they are owed something; that they are entitled to what they want. It is also the equivalent to a poverty mindset.

So what is the difference? Winners do what losers won't. They act consistently, they seek an edge through mentorship and books, applied effort and they pay the price in advance for what they want. They are fully committed!

"Winners focus on winning! Loser always focus on winners..." - Dr. Jerry Grillo

If you feel stuck in a job and can't leave despite entrepreneurial dreams, then you're more committed to security than wealth and growth.

If you read books about creating wealth or attend trainings, but your actions don't reflect what you've learned, then you're "interested in wealth." You aren't committed to creating it.

Without commitment, there's no action, and without action, there are no results.

Your commitment produces a force of energy that opens doors and creates possibilities that otherwise wouldn't have been there. You find opportunity where there previously was none. Your forward progress is powerful, directed, focused and creates desired results when you're committed. No other alternative is possible because you will do whatever it takes to get what you are committed to. Nothing less is acceptable. Becoming wealthy is no longer a question of "if," but "when."

A common mistake many inexperienced entrepreneurs make is thinking that commitment is something that happens once at the beginning of the journey and that's enough to carry them through. This is false and completely inaccurate!

Commitment to your purpose/calling must be continually renewed. It is going to take incredible focus and discipline. Neglect it, even for a few days, and it will begin to wither.

Commit to your purpose every day and take actions that demonstrate your commitment. Just look back and remember a time in your past when you knew you would reach your goal, no matter what! It wasn't a maybe, or possibly or hopefully. You had a commitment to your objective deep within your bones. Your faith was anchored in a belief that you would get it done no matter the cost, and you refused to settle for anything less than what you desired. It's within these actions that you prove your commitment. Words mean nothing without real demonstration of your commitment. Commitment ignites your actions. Becoming successful is no longer a question of "if," but "when."

Acquiring abundance as an entrepreneur demands that you be fully committed to being disciplined and accountable for your decisions and ACTIONS. Success demands that you have an UNWAVERING commitment to persevere despite the setbacks that life will throw your way. You will need to be committed to take CONSISTENT ACTION on a daily basis to see your desires fully manifested. You must believe that no matter what happens, no matter how badly you fail—and you will—that you pick yourself up after every failure and try once again. Refuse to stop or give in until you have reached your destination!

Solomon says in Ecclesiastes 9:10, *"Whatever your hand finds to do, do it with your might."* That is to say, whatever you do, do it to the best of your ability.

God highly prizes diligence.

"The precious possession of a [wise] man is diligence…" Proverbs 12:27 (Amplified Bible)

"The plans of the diligent lead surely to plenty (Abundance)." Proverbs 21:5 (Amplified Bible)

"A slack hand causes poverty, but the hand of the diligent makes rich." Proverbs 10:4 (English Standard Version)

In fact, God demands diligence!

"You shall diligently keep the commandments of the LORD your God." Deuteronomy 6:17 (English Standard Version)

In Deuteronomy 28:1 we read, *"If you diligently obey the voice of the LORD your God... the LORD your God will set you high above all nations of the earth."* Wealth is promised, victory is promised, but there's a requirement on our end to qualify for the rewards of God. The proof of your desire lies in your diligent persevering pursuit! Diligence is the consistent application of God's principles. The diligent walk in perpetual favor because their actions demand it.

A.) The Diligent are Rich.

"He becometh poor that dealeth with a slack hand: but the hand of the diligent maketh rich." Proverbs 10:4

B.) The Diligent have Authority.

"The hand of the diligent shall bear rule: but the slothful shall be under tribute." Proverbs 12:24

C. The Diligent think only Abundance.

"The thoughts of the diligent tend only to plenteousness; but of every one that is hasty only to want." Proverbs 21:5

Kevin Mullens

D. The Diligent obtain Favor.

"He that diligently seeketh good procureth favour: but he that seeketh mischief, it shall come unto him." Proverbs 11:27

Hebrews 11:6 shows us that God takes diligence seriously; *"He is a rewarder of those who diligently seek Him."* God can see who is serious about seeking Him. We are to strive for the goals that He sets for us. Your faith without works is dead. Ask, Seek, Knock are all avenues into accessing God's treasures, but they are all ACTIONS. So, if you truly want a promotion or to increase and advance, you must be DILIGENT! You must be willing to invest all of your energy in the things that are necessary to obtain your heart's desire!

You qualify for wealth, overflow, victory, deliverance and FAVOR when you arrive at greatness through all that you have endured instead of waiting for God to force you into it.

Favor is not the absence of work or effort; that wouldn't be favor that would be welfare! Favor increases your reward because of your efforts and ACTIONS. Stop saying, *"God is going to bless me,"* and realize He has ALREADY blessed you!

Your future is **unfolding by the power of your <u>expectations</u> and <u>diligence.</u>** Do not lose faith even if your desired future seems unobtainable. Abundance is coming!

"....for there is a sound of abundance of rain." 1 Kings 18:41

We often quote scriptures or affirmations that demand increase and ABUNDANCE, but we lose faith when it does not happen in our expected time. Notice Elijah heard the sound of abundance. Elijah sent his servant out to see what he heard and six times the servant came back and said, *"There is nothing."* But when he went the seventh time he saw a cloud.

"And it came to pass at the seventh time, that he said, Behold, there arise a little cloud out of the sea, like a man's hand." 1 Kings 18:44

Imagine Elijah's faith; he was promised rain in ABUNDANCE. Then he finally sees a cloud, but it is only the size of a man's hand. Elijah had great expectation and unwavering faith. He never doubted that abundance was coming. You have been promised wealth. You are applying a positive mindset daily. Your actions act in spite of your current reality. Then sometimes doubt sinks in, and we can't see wealth or abundance because we have a small results or even little to no results. Don't you ever let go of God's promise of "LIFE MORE ABUNDANTLY."

The Lord isn't satisfied with just blessing you. His very nature could be mistaken for wasteful... *"Pressed down, shaken and running over"* (Luke 6:38). What man calls waste, God calls Abundance.

"And the Lord shall make YOU have a "SURPLUS of prosperity," through the fruit of your body, of your livestock, and of your ground, in the land which the Lord swore to your fathers to give you." Deuteronomy 28:11 (Amplified Bible, Classic Edition)

In my book, *"Great Things Happen to Those Who Take Action,"* I talk about the power of speaking "I AM."

"I AM healed." "I AM wealthy." " I AM!!!!"

Whatever you say after "I AM" starts materializing. It is important that you apply the scriptures to your personal life instead of reading it like a history book.

"And the Lord shall make (put your name here) have a surplus of prosperity."

According to the Dictionary the word SURPLUS is defined as *"the amount that remains when use or need is satisfied." [ii]*

I love the way that sounds; the amount that remains after. That's a powerful explanation of SURPLUS.

"So shall thy barns be filled with PLENTY..." Proverbs 3:10

This is what surplus is; moving beyond even into overflow. This is the *More Than Enough* nature of God that positions your income to overflowing status. Re-read Deuteronomy 28:11, and you will see the blessing is a SURPLUS of PROSPERITY. Not just surplus but surplus of prosperity. Do not settle for just your needs being met. Accept God's promises and embrace your destiny.

Your faith and targeted action is manifesting momentum and exponential blessings even if you can't currently see it. Surplus of prosperity is arriving soon. Poverty will give way to prosperity.

"The sign of the hand in the sky, Elijah said, "That cloud, the size of a man's hand, like a vapor." What was it? It was that He believed. "I hear the sound of abundance of rain." That

cloud turn into two clouds. Two clouds become a hill, a hill become a mountain and the mountain, become another mountain; The next thing you know, the whole skies were thundering, rain was falling. What was it? He accepted what God sent!" -Prophet William Branham

Kevin Mullens

CHAPTER FIVE

BELIEVING!
The Internal Power To Succeed In An External World

"BELIEVE IT, BEHAVE IT, BECOME IT!" –
Dr. Cindy Trimm

In John chapter 5, Jesus was in Jerusalem for a festival, and walked into the area where the pool of Bethesda was located.

The pool of Bethesda was known for its healing properties, and for times when miraculous healing occurred as an angel would come down once a year and trouble the waters. John tells us, that it was here that a great number of disabled people used to lay—the blind, the lame, the paralyzed. One man had been there as an invalid for 38 years. When Jesus saw him lying there and learned that he had been in this condition for a long time, He asked him, *"Do you want to get well?"*

"Sir," the invalid replied, *"I have NO ONE TO HELP ME into the pool when the water is stirred. While I am trying to get in, someone else goes down ahead of me"* (John 5:1-7).

The attitude of this man towards the power of God for healing is interesting and seems to be how a lot of us operate both spiritually and naturally. We are in need of something, but often are waiting on someone else to help. Therefore, we remain paralyzed and rarely change.

All of his hopes were centered on this pool of limitation. Until the day Jesus walked by. Jesus said to him, *"Get up! Pick up your bed and walk."* At once the man was cured; he picked up his bed and walked (John 5:8-9).

Sometimes—through trials, circumstances or dry seasons—it can seem as though we have missed our blessing altogether. Maybe we are sitting by a "pool of limitation" like the man by the pool of Bethesda, waiting for a sign. God wants us to catch a fresh vision of His promised Word—to have faith and take action. You are not waiting on God. God is waiting on you!

This moment and day are filled with extraordinary possibilities. You are here right now to make the very most of them. So often we settle or sit around waiting on someone to rescue us. Be completely involved in this miracle of life and make the most of it. Remove self-imposed limitations and be free to live life unlimited.

One of the things that separate the seemingly favored from everyone else is their ability to take initiative—to do what needs to be done before anyone else recognizes it needs to be done. Initiative means "taking action" before the action is required or even necessary. It is the ability to do things without being told. Instead of waiting on the leader, you decide to be the best possible leader you can be! It means acting before understanding all the details. It means doing more than is expected!

Initiative is the willingness to own the outcome by taking full ownership. Being accountable! You always find initiative among all successful entrepreneurs. You see it in their personal development efforts, like their reading and studying to improve their leadership skills. No one has to tell them it is necessary. They just do it! You see it in their plan of action to set goals that would scare most and to direct their own work to achieve greater results than anyone requires or expects. They take initiative instead of relying on their mentors to tell them what they must do to succeed.

Taking initiative is the cornerstone in the foundation of leadership that gets results; it is acting proactively, not simply reacting. So you have to ask yourself; Are you waiting on God, the church or possibly the government to do what needs to be done? Or are you taking initiative? Do not wait for the perfect opportunity, but take the opportunity and make it perfect.

You have the opportunity, right here and now, to experience a positive, rich and fulfilling life. Why in the world would you ever choose to do anything else? Scripture says you can have life or death (Deuteronomy 30:19). CHOOSE LIFE!

IDENTITY

Be intentional about seeing yourself as God sees you. So

many still suffer with identity crisis, allowing their past or the opinions of others to restrain them from living a life of fulfillment. David was a sheepherder for his father, but he did not allow his role to define him. God's word and anointing upon his life would define him.

Maybe you have some things in common with David. David's brothers had voted him *"the least likely to be significant."* He wasn't even present the day that the Prophet Samuel came calling to ordain a king. Samuel, having the eyes of the Lord, knew when he saw David that he was looking upon the future king of Israel. Maybe you've felt left out or uninvited before. It doesn't matter how others sees you. God has rightly appointed you for a purpose and on purpose. You will start acting, speaking, and reflecting accordingly like sons and daughters of the King when you recognize your rightful position of authority!

David was belittled by his older brother on the day he first saw Goliath and pursued by King Saul as an outlaw; yet in God's due time he stepped into his destiny. There was no power that could hinder David's destiny. I don't care what things currently look like. I want you to realize that you have been ordained and called for such a time as this. Nothing other than your self-imposed limitations can ever hinder you.

Imagine this, David and his men returning to their homes and property in Ziklag, only to find that their homes had been burned, their property pillaged and destroyed and their wives and kids captured by the enemy while they were gone. To make matters worse, David's men turned against him and talked about stoning him to death; blaming him for the tragedy. We've all felt that blame before, but David encouraged himself in the Lord.

David could easily have thrown in the towel, given up and quit, but he stayed on track with his destiny and made tough leadership decisions. As a result, David and his men overcame the enemy, recovered their losses with interest and won back their families (1 Samuel 30).

The devastation of Ziklag prepared David for his move to Hebron—the very place where he would be crowned King of Judah and then of all Israel (2 Samuel 2).

Do you feel like you're undergoing the greatest trial of your life? I've always said that battle is inevitable as you advance your life and that warfare is always a sign that your enemy has discerned your future. Be strong in faith and recognize the value within your trial, as it is typically the launch pad of your next promotion. Problems are invitations to rewards.

Your immediate reality is a chance for you to show your faithfulness and display your leadership as you are transitioning for a season of uncommon Favor.

"But as for you, be strong and DO NOT GIVE UP, for your work will be rewarded." 2 Chronicles 15:7 NIV

Winning is a habit. Unfortunately, so is quitting. As parents, we often remind our kids that if they start something, like music lessons or sports, quitting is not an option. It's because we know the value of finishing. However, as adults, we often lend every excuse on why we can't do something. There is a scripture that says, *"No one who puts his hand to the plow and looks back is fit for service in the kingdom of God"* (Luke 9:62)NIV.

We were ordained and created to be blessed so we can be a

blessing, but success requires sacrifice, focus and unusual determination. Remember, that you can become bitter OR become BETTER when faced with circumstances you feel inadequate to handle. How easy do you get distracted after setting a goal? How easy do you give up when it gets hard? How fast do you tap out when life has pinned you down? I'm here to tell you that you are closer than you think. The things you fear are tricks of the enemy designed to paralyze you from moving forward and living in the Promised Land. The pain, discomfort and minor defeats are only temporary setbacks that you can learn from. Create character and recognize your warrior status. Challenge yourself to push harder when 'quit' comes knocking, and you'll soon find yourself at your desired destiny! How? Keep going! When you have a long way to go, keep going. When you've almost reached the goal, keep going.

Success is achieved by those who simply do whatever it takes to keep going. Pick yourself up again and again, and keep going. You know full well that you can do it, so do it. Remind yourself why you've chosen to get there, and just keep going.

"And let us not be weary in well doing: for in due season we shall reap, IF WE FAINT NOT." Galatians 6:9

"Persistence and determination alone are omnipotent. The slogan 'PRESS ON' has solved and always will solve the problems of the human race." - Calvin Coolidge

"The world ain't all sunshine and rainbows. It's a very mean and nasty place and I don't care how tough you are; it will beat you to your knees and keep you there permanently if you let it. You, me, or nobody is gonna hit as hard as life. But it

ain't about how hard ya hit. It's about how hard you can get hit and keep moving forward." - Rocky Balboa

Success is not a secret. Success is a process and a way of life. Success is not merely something that you get. Success is all about the way you choose to live. Success is the journey, and not merely the end of the road. It is about experiencing every moment as an opportunity to live the success you seek. Dream without limits, and ACT on those dreams. Live without excuses and with a persistent, burning desire to make a difference; never compromise your life with mediocrity but raise your standards and level of expectation.

Success is a WAY OF LIFE. It starts with a thought and then it consumes our actions. Choose that way of thinking and acting right now, and in every moment of every day. Rise above feelings of inadequacy and remove self-damaging beliefs. Choose Life. Choose Success.

The more tuned in you are to your purpose, and the more dedicated you are to growing toward it, the better your chances of reaching your potential, expanding your possibilities, and doing something significant.

"To reach your full potential you must grow, and to grow, you must be highly intentional about it. Growth compounds and accelerates if you remain intentional about it." - John C Maxwell

Anybody can remain where they are and become subject to life's limitations; but to those who are dissatisfied and commit to a life of growth, your best days are ahead of you! The chains of procrastination and complacency are broken. In the midst of God creating the universe, He looked down and realized He needed one of you. God has invested in you. Your God dream may seem impossible or even magical, but the magical becomes material when your inspiration is backed by action and unusual determination. Anybody can, but will you?

We all know how it feels to stand still in fear or to become paralyzed when confronted with an obstacle we believe is too hard to overcome, and to often the greatest enemy we face is ourselves. To many times we give in to that inner chump that says, *"Who do you think you are?"* or, *"Why even try because you know you will fail. It is just too hard."* The voice of complacency says you should back away from anything that will require sacrifice and temporary pain. You will have to lean on WILL POWER in order to move to the next level. Now do not get the wrong idea, I am not placing will power separate from the power of God within you. Every child of God has access to the same God, but too many sit around waiting on God when it is God waiting on them. That is like praying for an 'A' on a test when you only studied for a 'B,' or asking God to move a mountain when you're unwilling to pick up a shovel. The Christian's motto should not be 'Let go and let God' or 'If it's God's will.' but rather 'Trust God and get going!' God's favor tends to show up in the life of the DOER.

"There are things that God can't do. HE can't answer a prayer you don't pray and HE can't bless a work you don't do." - Paul Orberson

Every achievement is an idea that has been acted upon. A single idea can end up being worth millions of dollars especially if it is a GOD-IDEA. Yet for that to happen, it cannot remain just an idea. Consistent focused action is the way wishes and intentions are transformed into results and achievements. Don't keep your greatest possibilities locked away in your thoughts. Bring those dreams and possibilities to life with your actions. Complacent people die with their dreams locked within. They bury their talents in the ground. Dissatisfied people choose to do what is necessary to move their thought life to material life.

When you have a great idea, act on it, now and for as long as it takes to bring it decisively to life.

Dissatisfied people don't wait for things to happen. They use their words and actions to create and make things happen. There is a fire in their belly that fuels their passion and launches them into the deep waters of endless possibilities. Will power is the ability to arrive at a DECISION and follow it through with perseverance and consistency until it's a successful accomplishment. You must go beyond just saying, *"Greater is He that lives within me than my trials."* or *"I can do ALL things through CHRIST who strengthens me."* When you make a DECISION you will either FIND a way or MAKE a way!

There is a proverb that says, *"Great souls have wills; feeble ones have only wishes."* We have an *Infinite Source* that lives within us that does not believe in the impossible. Too many have defied the odds, amazed doctors, and survived impossible odds by using WILL POWER. When you discipline your thoughts and truly determine within yourself to find a way, then mountains become hills and fears disappear. WILL POWER starts in the mind and once acted upon, it brings everything under its authority. Your limitations are only what you allow them to be. You are much stronger than you believe. You are predestined for greatness. Do not compromise! Your authentic purpose is too important to settle. Lean on WILL

POWER to catapult you into your promised destiny through your relentless efforts and faith in God to see you through when you feel like quitting or disappointment has distracted you. Remind yourself that life is not merely happening to you, but that life is happening through you. You are worthy of the best life has to give because you are able to give your very best. Let go of all the limitations you have placed on yourself and accept the miracle of your existence.

"...But this one thing I do, forgetting those things which are behind, and reaching forth unto those things which are before, I press toward the mark for the prize of the high calling of God in Christ Jesus." Philippians 3:13-14

CHAPTER SIX

THE DISSATISFIED! Are Committed To A Lifetime Of Growth

The Law for More Is Hidden in What You Already Have!

There was a time when people believed that the world was flat? That belief become their personal doctrine and determined how they viewed the world. It didn't matter that the world was really round. They believed it was flat, and that belief influenced their version of the real world.

OUR BELIEFS CONTROL OUR LIVES.

We love to customize the facts to fit our internal belief system; how we view opportunity, God, family, science, money, etc. We force things to fit what we believe so we don't have to change or get uncomfortable.

If we have created a belief system where "opportunity" is everywhere, that's what we will always see. When our belief system is based on opportunity and the positive, we don't view challenges as obstacles because that wouldn't harmonize with our belief system.

Successful entrepreneurs see the same things you do, but they see them differently. So we interpret things in a way that allow them to support our internal belief system, which determines our reality. If you ever catch that you will begin to attract success like a huge magnet drawing all that is good towards you.

When you can look back on your journey to where you are now, can see how your commitment to personal growth begins to build your belief system and change how you feel about wealth or your self-worth? This also allows insight into where others are as you lead, mentor and train them.

Any area in our life where we are producing good results is probably anchored to an empowering belief without limitations. Any area in our life that is consumed with frustrating results is likely anchored to a limiting belief that you are struggling with. Many self-sabotage before they ever get started, because of their belief system.

The results we produce ALWAYS reveal our beliefs. Now you can re-evaluate where you are and the results you are getting and determine if your belief system needs changed.

"For with God NOTHING SHALL BE IMPOSSIBLE." Luke 1:37

The difference between a successful person and an

unsuccessful person is in their "THOUGHT LIFE." Thoughts become words, and words are life and death. Thoughts determine the actions we take. People who are always happy, joyful and positive have chosen to look on the brighter side of things, even in some of the worse cases imaginable. They live with an unconquered mind and refuse to be persuaded by the voice of self-pity, complaint or negativity. They have recognized that their dominant thoughts become their reality.

Negative people have chosen to think and meditate on all of the bad things that can happen or go wrong in life. No matter what good may come their way, they will often overlook it because they are focused only on the bad. As a result of all of this negative thinking in their thought process, they self-sabotage and never attract the many blessings they are entitled to.

Take your thoughts CAPTIVE, or they'll take you captive. We are in a constant battle within our mind as we live in a chaotic world that's constantly feeding us with everything negative. Often people become addicted to this morbid thought life and stay in a constant depressed state. But this is a battle you can win. Especially when you take on the mind of Christ.

"For though we walk in the flesh, we do not war according to the flesh. For the weapons of our warfare are not carnal but mighty in God for pulling down strongholds, casting down arguments and every high thing that exalts itself against the knowledge of God, bringing EVERY THOUGHT into CAPTIVITY to the obedience of Christ." 2 Corinthians 10:3-5

Your reality can be whatever you want it to be. There are no limits to what you can achieve. Barriers in your way are but illusions that are creations of negative and fearful thought. Often things are not as difficult as they seem.

There may be times when it seems the whole world is working against you. Yet in reality, the main thing working against you is your own negative perception or thinking. When one thing goes wrong, then another and another, it probably seems to you that you're having a bad day. Keep in mind, however, that it's just your perception. Whatever you focus on will expand.

Instead of using your energy to build and maintain a negative perception, put that energy into creating positive results. You are stronger and much more capable than any circumstance that you may be encountering. With determination and action, you can break free and experience victory. Although life is filled with great challenges, the world is not conspiring against you. Even when one disappointment is followed by another and another, you are not having a bad day.

The primary function of life is not to simply survive; especially when Jesus came that you might have life MORE ABUNDANTLY (John 10:10). You are capable of way more; you are capable of living and accomplishing the extraordinary. You are here to do something meaningful, to passionately engage with life and to thrive. Your life is filled with endless possibilities. And you can think, talk and act right now in a positive way, to bring the very best of those possibilities to life.

UFC fighter Conor McGregor, who was once broke and collecting welfare checks in Dublin, did the seemingly impossible and knocked out Jose Aldo in 13 seconds of the first round. Aldo had not lost in 10 years. Since that time,

Conor has become the highest paid per view draw in the UFC, and has a net worth estimated at $25 million dollars. Plus, he is the first simultaneously two weight-class champion in UFC history. Pay close attention to what McGregor's said after the fight.

"This is the law of attraction. When things are going good and you visualize these good things, that's easy. What's not easy to do is when things are going bad, and you're visualizing the good stuff. And that was what I was able to do. Even though I was having these troubles at home, and even though I had no job, and nothing was happening, I was still able to feel like it was. I was like a kid using my imagination. Driving in my girlfriend's little car; a little Peugeot 206 shaking down the road, I was visualizing my success. I'm sitting at the steering wheel visualizing a brand new car, visualizing good things in times of struggle. And when you can do that, that's really what makes the law of attraction work. It really attracts the fortune to you more, when you're in the struggle and still visualizing these things."[iii]

McGregor's reference to the law of attraction is the mantra – *"As a man thinks in his heart, so is he" (Proverbs 23:7)*, or "I think, therefore I am." It is the mental practice and exercise of firmly believing, visualizing and flooding your thoughts with that which your heart desires. It alludes to the fact that all physical manifestations in life first begin as a thought—a belief within the subconscious. The seeds of true materialization of ones goals and dreams must first be planted in the human psyche before they can ever materialize into physical reality. Think of McGregor gripping the steering wheel of his girlfriend's car while visualizing a new one (Vision Board). His vision manifested into existence. By thought something is brought to you, and by action is it received!

We are all the product of our thoughts. The omnipotent power that lives within you will always manifest your dominant thoughts.

LAW OF ATTRACTION IN SCRIPTURE

"Finally, brethren, whatsoever things are true, whatsoever things are honest, whatsoever things are just, whatsoever things are pure, whatsoever things are lovely, whatsoever things are of good report; if there be any virtue, and if there be any praise, THINK on these things." Philippians 4:8

The New American Standard version says, "DWELL on these things…" which also means meditate.

"For as he THINKETH in his heart, so IS he…" Proverbs 23:7

Of course, you are already very familiar with this scripture. God has always taught the believer the power of positive thinking and having the right mental attitude.

"Good man out of the good treasure of his heart bringeth forth that which is good; and an evil man out of the evil treasure of his heart bringeth forth that which is evil: for of the abundance of the heart his mouth speaketh." Luke 6:45

The outward is a direct reflection of the inward. You self-sabotage your rightful heritage to wealth when your heart and mindset disbelieves. Abundance, prosperity and wealth must be something you accept as your divine right. When you believe that you are already wealthy and you remain focused on what's rightfully yours, then it can flow towards you naturally and effortlessly. You are a magnificent creator that was made in the image of the Master Creator. Guard your thoughts, words and belief system because the subconscious ultimately determines your actions, and your actions determine what you get.

For years athletes couldn't run one mile in under four minutes. Even doctors said it was physically impossible. Roger Bannister silenced the internal and external voices that said, "It can't be done." He ran a mile under four minutes, proving that the human heart could hold up in such conditions. This courageous act inspired others who quickly even broke Roger's record.

The belief that no one could run a mile in under four minutes was conquered. There is also the story of Olympic champion, Vasily Alexeev, who broke the weight lifting barrier of 500 pounds. This was thought to be an impossible feat reserved for fairy tales. Yet before he could accomplish it himself, Alexeev's trainers changed his limiting belief by rigging 501.5 pounds of weights to look like 499. WOW! The mind is so powerful and whatever our dominant thoughts are, will always manifest our reality. [iv]

There is the incredible story of Wilma Rudolph who was paralyzed as a child. She had every right to question WHY this had to happen to her. She could have completely given up and lived with a victim mentality, but her will to overcome her circumstances was greater than the circumstance itself.

At the age of four, she was paralyzed after being hit by infantile paralysis (among other deadly illnesses such as double pneumonia and scarlet fever). The doctors told Wilma's mom that she'd never walk again, at least not like a normal child would walk. The positive voice of her momma said she would walk again.

Whose voice influences you?

Wilma NEVER GAVE UP. She pressed on and struggled to walk with her steel brace until she could eventually walk without it; which amazed even her doctors! Wilma pushed her limits and removed boundaries to the point where she could not only walk without a limp, but she could run. At 16, she joined her high school track team and went from the girl who always limped to the girl who won every single race she entered.

It wasn't long before Wilma was selected to represent America during the Olympics in three events. She took on what was once thought impossible! Wilma became the first American woman in U.S. history to win three gold medals in track during a single Olympic Game in the 1960 Summer Olympics. It is said that she achieved that on a sprained ankle. She became known as *"The Tornado, the fastest woman on earth."*

Yes, we're talking about the girl who was paralyzed as a child, but through perseverance, determination and FAITH she regained her ability to walk and run—to the point where she could outrun people who were born healthy without any disability. She out ran other countries elite athletes that were handpicked to win the gold. [v]

Believe in yourself! Keep investing in your dreams and

someday you to will recognize that you control your destiny.

Your belief system will decide the limits you set for yourself and what you can and deserve to achieve. If you believe you are a person who cannot succeed, then success will escape you. You will subconsciously create ways to self-destruct because of what you believe about yourself. If you believe you are a person who can succeed, then you will act in such a way to make it happen!

Do not allow others to tell you what can and cannot do. Wilma found comfort and strength in the voice of her mother. Words are life and death so be mindful of who you communicate with when facing adverse conditions. Rename moments of perceived defeat and begin labeling moments from a positive perspective.

King David understood how powerful words were when he and his men went out, full of faith, and were victorious over the Philistines. The Bible says that David renamed the valley. Instead of calling it the valley of giants, which meant the valley of Rephaim; he renamed it Baal-perazim; which means *"The God of the Breakthrough."*

Most people make very poor language choices. They fail to recognize the power of conversation. They will use disempowering phrases like, "I'm doing alright," or "I'm okay." They'll tell you that they "Hate Mondays," or say things like, "I'm glad it is hump-day," or "Thank God it is Friday." Statements that further validate how miserable life can be when you are just surviving. Who wants to be just "okay?" That sounds like the exact opposite of the life God promised.

Entrepreneurs are different. Their language produces meaningful experiences and life without limits. If you ask them how they are, they will say things like, "Amazing!" or "Wonderful!" or "Highly Favored." They tell you that they are "Dominating," or "Changing the world," and "Living in abundance." They use words to design their life. They understand that they are the architect of their destiny. You'll never hear a top performer say that they are "Just happy to be above ground."

Your life is not an excuse for compromise. It is not selfish or greedy to want to achieve more. What is selfish is to accept less than what you can be. Break generational curses, walls, barriers and limitations that stand between you and your dreams coming true. Stop following the map laid out by the masses and go create your own map.

You can waste time brainwashing yourself with the disempowering belief that the economy or other circumstances are responsible for your lackluster results. You deny yourself the gift of your own resilience and your ability to find a way with this way of thinking. Those that take 100% responsibility for their life will always find a way and make a way!

It's true that taking 100% responsibility for your life and your results is a scary proposition. Owning up to your failures is one of the great attributes of true leadership. Those that don't make excuses and take responsibility look to their losses and failures for lessons.

Maybe you think…
- Your town is tough…. *I've seen worse.*
- You don't have enough resources.
- Nobody likes you.

- You are not properly trained.
- You don't have influence.

IT DOESN'T MATTER!

If you believe that the past events of your life are in any way responsible for your results, then you deny yourself your future. Stop allowing your history to determine your destiny. Let go of every belief that is rooted in blame. Even if you believe that the events of your past are even one percent to blame. Get rid of self-imposed limitations that are destroying your ability to take action.

I can point to people who are very successful because they took one hundred percent responsibility for producing the results that they desire. I know people who experienced a horrible childhood that could have just collapsed and stayed down, but are now successful and happy because they took one hundred percent responsibility for their lives. You know these stories and others like them. You may even have one of your own.

What's the area of your life that restrains and paralyzes you from moving forward that you need to reclaim now so that you can empower yourself by taking one hundred percent responsibility for your life and ultimately your results?

Examine your belief system (mindset) because whatever you believe determines how you act. Everything in your future will be the manifestation from your current beliefs. So make sure you identify roadblocks and self-imposed limitations.

The state that you create within you will determine your behavior, which will determine your outcomes. Your belief system determines whether you see opportunities or problems. Your inner dialogue determines whether you feel empowered or disempowered, but clarity comes the moment you know who you are. You are the expressed thoughts of almighty God. You are royalty! You are a winner! You are relentless, resourceful and resilient! The critics outside are no match for the champion inside! Today, you win!

CHAPTER SEVEN

INCREASE!
The Result Of Applying What God Has Deposited In You

The "talents" in the parable of talents does not refer to singing, artistic talent and the like. Although we are blessed with many different talents and how we develop our God given talent determines our usefulness; however the talent in this parable is a weight of gold. Currency! Matthew 25:18 calls it the "Lord's money." This parable was less about salvation and more about making the most of our earthly calling.

"...Master, I know you have high standards and hate careless ways, that you demand the best and make no allowances for error." Matthew 25:24 (Message Bible)

The parable of talents teaches us that God invests in people, not business ideas. He never asked to see their business plan.

He only expected INCREASE. God invests in people. God doesn't pour out His oil on systems, but on people. The Kingdom of God is within us. You will better understand the longing in your heart to make a difference—to create—when you fully understand that God poured Himself into people. God placed that desire inside of you.

Notice in the parable that God allocated money to the servants according to their potential and abilities to create increase. You may be a one-talent person or a five-talent person. This is not a competition with others; it is about you growing yourself, sharpening your skills and learning to thrive in your gift zone. Whatever you are capable of doing, DO IT with ALL YOUR MIGHT.

As you invest in yourself, grow and become MORE, you begin to attract the most positive things into your life. Your bank account will grow as the direct result of how you grow. Jesus said in Matthew 5:16 "...*let your light shine before others, so that they may see your good works and give glory to your Father who is in heaven.*"

If you don't see the need to invest in brightening your light, then you might not be cut out for the entrepreneurial lifestyle. If you want your business to succeed, take care of your mind, body and soul. Your "BEST BUSINESS" will depend on the level of the "BEST YOU." Have you hit a wall, stopped growing, experienced loss of motivation or feeling stuck? Here's the good news...you can get back up and kick it in high gear again, experiencing full throttle momentum.

The greatest tragedy is not living up to your full potential. Sometimes we are just in the wrong environment or under the wrong leadership. If you are a five-talent person serving under

(70)

the administration of one-talent leadership, then you will never grow.

The servants that were praised in the parable of talents were those who made maximum profit with the investment that was given to them. Do not think for a minute that you will not be held accountable for the talents God has placed in your life.

A parable is told about a man who had a fig tree in his garden. He watched this tree for three years, but it never produced any fruit. He called for the dresser of the vineyard and told him to cut down the tree. It was fruitless; therefore it was useless. It looked like a fig tree, but had no figs (Luke 13:6-7).

This sounds harsh, but understand that we are to bear forth fruit if we have the spirit of Christ within us; not only joy, love and peace, but also abundance and increase. You can go to church, read the Bible, attend empowerment seminars, study Kingdom principles and have the knowledge, but not have any fruit that bears witness. Theoretical knowledge is one thing. You must apply the knowledge. You must stir up the gift within you, and let every area of your life bear witness that you are a child of the King; not a king but THE KING!

In the parable, the master had a problem with the servant who made no profit. Wicked/Slothful is what the Lord called this servant. Stop assassinating your chances of obtaining wealth through a belief that money is somehow bad.

God is not against the profit motive. "Wanting money" isn't the same as being "money-motivated." Never apologize for wanting to create wealth or live prosperous. Money has never been evil or God would not have said that He takes pleasure in the prosperity of His servants (Psalm 35:27), or that the blessings of the Lord makes rich (Proverbs 10:22). Your heavenly Father desires that you would prosper and have an abundant life (John 10:10).

Everyone wants more money. The difference between simply "wanting money" and being "motivated" by money is understanding the freedom it can provide and the willingness to take the actions necessary to get it. People that only want money are usually not willing to do the work that is necessary.

Don't misinterpret what I am saying. I am not talking about the love of money. I'm talking about being at peace with your desire to be wealthy. The amount of money you earn is directly proportional to the value that you create for other people. Little value, little money. Massive value, massive money. Small actions, little results. Massive actions, massive results.

The more people you serve, the more money you make. The more people that benefit from your work, the more you earn. The more people you help become successful directly reflects how successful you become. The freedom-motivated know this law and take relentless action. Money isn't everything. People that make money their master instead of their servant are never happy. If you want money, you'll never have it. If you are motivated enough to work harder than others are willing to in the most productive areas, then money will find its way to you and do so abundantly!

Walk away from scarcity mindset. Poverty is a disease and money is the cure. Money is a tool that can build, advance and influence nations for the glory of God in the hands of believers.

Money takes on the personality of its master. From this day forward choose to partner with leadership that encourages you and trains you to multiply your talents and bring forth increase.

Notice the scriptures concerning the unprofitable servant:

"His lord answered and said unto him, Thou wicked and slothful servant, thou knewest that I reap where I sowed not, and gather where I have not strawed: Thou oughtest therefore to have put my money to the exchangers, and then at my coming I should have received mine own with usury. Take therefore the talent from him, and give it unto him which hath ten talents. For unto every one that hath shall be given, and he shall have abundance: but from him that hath not shall be taken away even that which he hath. And cast ye the unprofitable servant into outer darkness: there shall be weeping and gnashing of teeth." Matthew 25:26-30

The master reallocated the funds. God will move financial favor to the hands of the diligent. Solomon said, *"The hand of the diligent make the rich" (Proverbs 10:4).* It would seem strange on the surface that the master gave the talent that was buried in the ground to the most profitable servant. Maybe you are wondering why He didn't give it to the poor? The investor understood His talent (money) is seed, and seed has a responsibility to bring a harvest.

"To him that has shall more be given abundance..."

The most profitable of the servants turned five into ten. He obviously was first rewarded according to his abilities, but ability is useless if not used. He was not only capable, but through effort and wisdom, he doubled his Lord's money. Everything given to you by God is in its raw state. It is your responsibility to harness and develop it; it is negligent and irresponsible if you do not.

"So then every one of us shall give account of himself to God." Romans 14:12

Do not overlook the judgment of the servant who buried his Lord's investment. He was labeled wicked. It wasn't so much that he wasted the master's money, but he wasted the opportunity. His fate was to be cast into outer darkness.

It is time we stop pretending there is no judgment for sitting on unused potential. We have made wealth and success so unrighteous that it has become an accepted doctrine that we should live on just enough or do just enough. That kind of thinking landed the unprofitable servant in eternal punishment. If you will not do it then God will raise up someone that will. You are blessed with Godly gifts so stop renting out your gift for a wage. Decide to unleash your full potential and enlarge your capacity. Launch into the deep where abundance is waiting on you. Let others remain complacent and content with mediocrity, but not you. Let others live in the land of not enough or never enough, but not you. Live daily with the highest of expectations that through your God given ability you can experience "MORE THAN ENOUGH."

GOD IS A BUSINESSMAN

God is a compassionate and merciful Father; God is also a businessman. You don't need to do anything for salvation. Simply surrender your heart to Father God and make him Lord of your life. Salvation is a finished work that you only need to accept. God, the businessman, provides principles and guidelines to Kingdom success that will cause you to inherit

Godly wealth. Knowing God does not create wealth; knowing and faithfully applying His principles does!

We can see the promise of God's Word are two fold—whether we are studying Deuteronomy 28, the book of Proverbs or great leaders within the scriptures that were wealthy. One is believing and declaring it. The second is acting upon it. If you ACT then God will ACT. It's time we infiltrate the market place and become influencers. Through success, we create platforms outside the church that demand people listen to us. As spirit filled entrepreneurs, we fill roles not only within the church, but also outside the church.

We have placed emphasis on every form of ministry possible from evangelism to worship to children's ministry, but there is also ministry in business. Everyone cannot preach, but everyone can own their own business or run for office. Everyone can choose to be significant and add value to the community. We become self-sufficient through a multitude of businesses. We can become the lender as the scriptures suggest instead of borrowing and living in debt. There is definitely a business side to God, and it demands profit. He has invested Himself in you. What will you do with His investment?

The money that was given to the servants in the parable of the talents was not their own. That would be like saying the tithe is the Lords, and the rest is mine. No! It is all the Lords. He is generous to those who are good stewards. The money the servants earned with the capital was not theirs to keep; they were only caretakers. It was the quality of their stewardship that the master wanted to measure. Bury your talents, and you get "weeping and gnashing of teeth." The choice is yours.

I CALL YOU BLESSED!

"And it shall come to pass, if thou shalt hearken diligently unto the voice of the LORD thy God, to observe and to do all his commandments which I command thee this day, that the LORD thy God will set thee on high above all nations of the earth: And all these blessings shall come on thee, and overtake thee, if thou shalt hearken unto the voice of the LORD thy God. BLESSED shalt thou be in the city, and BLESSED shalt thou be in the field. BLESSED shall be the fruit of thy body, and the fruit of thy ground, and the fruit of thy cattle, the increase of thy kine, and the flocks of thy sheep. BLESSED shall be thy basket and thy store. BLESSED shalt thou be when thou comest in, and BLESSED shalt thou be when thou goest out. The LORD shall cause thine enemies that rise up against thee to be smitten before thy face: they shall come out against thee one way, and flee before thee seven ways. The LORD shall command the blessing upon thee in thy storehouses, and in all that thou settest thine hand unto; and he shall BLESS thee in the land which the LORD thy God giveth thee. The LORD shall establish thee an holy people unto himself, as he hath sworn unto thee, if thou shalt keep the commandments of the LORD thy God, and walk in his ways. And all people of the earth shall see that thou art called by the name of the LORD; and they shall be afraid of thee. And the LORD shall make thee plenteous in goods, in the fruit of thy body, and in the fruit of thy cattle, and in the fruit of thy ground, in the land which the LORD sware unto thy fathers to give thee. The LORD shall open unto thee his good treasure, the heaven to give the rain unto thy land in his season, and to bless all the work of thine hand: and thou shalt lend unto many nations, and thou shalt not borrow. And the LORD shall make thee the head, and not the tail; and thou shalt be above only, and thou shalt not be beneath; if that thou hearken unto the commandments of the LORD thy God, which I command thee this day, to observe and to do them: And thou shalt not go aside from any of the words which I command thee this day, to the right hand, or to the left, to go after other gods to serve them." Deuteronomy 28:1-14

Deuteronomy 28 is a powerful chapter filled with promises. Notice the entire chapter hinged on obeying an instruction. The quickest way to get God INVOLVED in your Desires, Dreams, Plans is…

"In all thy ways acknowledge Him, and He shall DIRECT thy paths." Proverbs 3:6

"Commit your actions to the LORD, and your PLANS WILL SUCCEED." Proverbs 16:3 NLT

"Commit your way to the LORD; trust in Him, and He will ACT." Psalms 37:5 (English Standard Version)

"Keep this Book of the Law always on your lips; meditate on it Day and Night, so that you may be careful to do EVERYTHING written in it. Then you will be PROSPEROUS and SUCCESSFUL." Joshua 1:8 NIV

We have all sinned and fallen short in our journey to live for God. That is why His grace is sufficient. Many believers remain poor or live in the land of not enough when they serve a God whose very desire is for them to live in INCREASE and ABUNDANCE (Jeremiah 29:11).

Getting God involved in your dreams accelerates the process exponentially and multiplies what you cannot do on your own. Joseph, Solomon, Joshua and so many leaders in the Bible understood this, and God's men and women today walking in favor, truly understand this simple formula as well. Meditate upon these scriptures and see the power in their simplicity. Lay your request before Him and ask Him to manifest these desires with expectation and faith while you acknowledge Him in all you do.

Follow the instructions. God doesn't give advice. He gives instructions. The secret in seeing promises manifested is in your willingness to follow instructions. The Bible says, *"Poverty and shame shall be to him that refuseth instruction..."* (Proverbs 13:18). Let God mentor you. Partner with Him and watch your life transition into UNSTOPPABLE INCREASE.

CHAPTER EIGHT

GOALS!
Are Time Dated Dreams

When your current reality is radically different from where you want to be, goal setting will guarantee you reach your desired destiny.

Goals Shine When Radical Change IS Needed.

What is goal setting? It is taking a dream that seems unreal or unobtainable and moving toward it. Your goals are a representation of your inner desires; they allow you to tap into your true potential and stretch beyond average and ordinary and reach new heights. Your written and very clear goals ensure that you become the very best you can be to get the very best that life has to offer. You must write them down in order to give them life! Give your goals a deadline, and you will give your goals a voice.

How are you supposed to manifest what you truly want in life if you don't set concrete goals? How are you supposed to achieve your dreams and visions if you don't clearly set goals with the end result you desire? It is then that you can funnel your energy towards a specific target so your actions are producing the results you need to achieve your goals. It makes you crystallize the desires floating in your mind. It makes you live life on purpose and intentional.

Everything in this world is created twice. It is created in your mind first then it is manifested in reality. There will be no physical creation without mental creation. Thought life takes on a material life when you set a goal. I am encouraging you to stretch yourself and set bigger goals that require more from you than ever before. You will soon find that those things you previously thought were inadequate to accomplish have become your new normal.

Results Oriented

If you are "results oriented," you tend to see the end result very clearly, and you are looking for the "fastest" way to get there. You ask questions like…

- How can I achieve this?
- What do I have to do to get there?
- Do I have a *'whatever it takes'* mentality?

You want to have the result and the fulfillment that comes with it. You become much more focused on actions that "flow" towards the result you desire. You become very disciplined in your daily routine because you have begun to identify the things that get results and the things that waste time and energy. You understand how easy it is to get distracted and off your course; so you are laser focused and refuse to settle!

You already know what you need to do in order to reach your goals. The question is will you do what you know needs to be done to ensure success? You can indulge in self-development through reading and mentorship, and you will improve your leadership skills, increasing your ability and effectiveness as a business builder. WILL YOU commit to becoming more so you can be more, do more and earn more? You already know you need to Take Massive Immediate Action! WILL YOU?

"WILL YOU?"

Successful people are possessed with an "intense desire." It isn't that they always have the talent or skill. More often than not, it is simply that they have the WILL/DRIVE/AMBITION to take the little actions every day that less successful people aren't willing to take. They are obsessed about autographing their work with excellence. Those little actions taken daily eventually turn into big changes and eventually momentum. You know you need to apply the things you have read and learned. You know you need to get out of your comfort zone and go live life without limits. But "WILL YOU?"

Good Intentions versus Goals

Your good intentions are often meaningless. Actions are what matters most; not intentions.

Have you ever heard the saying, *"The road to Hell is paved with good intentions?"*

It's nice that you intended to make your prospecting calls, to fill up your calendar with appointments and reach your goals, but few have the self-discipline to take action. Therefore, few produce the outcomes they say they desire. It is your actions that produce your outcomes; not your good intentions.

Forget your good intentions and go guarantee yourself the results you seek by having the focus and discipline to take consistent action. Don't just intend to do the work you know needs to be done. Put it on the calendar; hold yourself accountable and TAKE ACTION. Put your goals in writing and add a deadline because your good intentions are often empty promises. It's your actions that produce the outcomes you need. Great things come to those who TAKE ACTION!

Becoming a Champion

Champions of anything do not just get lucky. They don't just talk about their goals as most do. They set challenging goals and go after them with courage and unusual determination. Self-sacrifice and discipline are more than words to the champion. They are a way of life. They understand that what they focus on EXPANDS. Champions overcome laziness and procrastination by setting meaningful and challenging goals. They then execute their plan of action with continual effort to ensure success.

Champions generally assess their goals differently from the average mindset by asking questions like, *"How bad do I really want this goal?" "Is the goal worth the price I'll have to pay physically, emotionally and spiritually?" "Is this goal in alignment with my belief system?" "Will I do whatever it takes?"*

If the answers to these questions are yes, champions close off all excuses and find a way to win. They decide, then commit and then go after it with fearless activity. They keep running the race until they cross the finish line. They understand that there will be times they are exhausted and want to quit, but they dig deep and push through the temporary pain to endure till the end.

Will they fail? Yes! Champions learn to "fail forward" and get back into the race. The champion knows there's no time for a pity party. Hesitation has no place in the champion's mindset. Champions get back into the race with courage and determination.

The champion doesn't give fifty percent of their time to their goals. They don't give seventy-five percent effort. The champion, the winner, always gives a hundred percent to their goals! They do not wish for success. They work for success. Many have a desire to have; few have the will to do it. There's a big difference between wanting to and willing too.

What Do You Want?

Essential to every journey is a destination. Ask any successful entrepreneur, and they will probably tell you how important it is to know exactly where you want to be at very specific points in time. You do this instead of walking aimlessly in circles, wasting your precious time.

ALICE IN WONDERLAND

"Would you tell me please which way I ought to go from here?" asked Alice

"That depends a good deal on where you want to get to." said the Cat

"I don't much care where." said Alice

"Then it doesn't matter which way you go." said the Cat

A lot of us can probably relate to this. We often want directions before we even know our exact destination. Life is full of surprises, so the path you are on might change; but it is always a good idea to know exactly where you are going when you are starting out. I know this might sound obvious, but so many people I meet are on a journey with no direction in mind. You have to know what your desired destiny is so you can visualize, focus and create a path built on massive action to guarantee you arrive exactly where you want. You are probably not going to end up where you want to be if you do not know where you want to go.

You must be specific when dreaming or even praying. There's a difference between aimlessly taking action and taking targeted action.

Prayer: *"I want to make more money."*

If you ask God for more money and you received a dollar then your request was granted. The MIND is DESIGNED to FOCUS on DEFINITE Goals and REPEL VAGUENESS. The omnipotent power of Almighty God living within you will materialize your dominant thoughts.

Prayer: *"I want one million dollars."*

This is something you can focus on, expect and plan. Dream in detail so your prayers or vision are not VAGUE; be very specific and don't think small. Create it in your mind.

"I want a home in Northern Ireland overlooking the Cliffs of Moher with cypress floors, black granite tops, an endless pool

overlooking the ocean, all stainless Samsung appliances, right on down to the color of each wall or the items on a desk."

This applies to reaching achievements, like winning a Grammy or writing a bestselling book. I'm just painting a picture that will help you understand the value of description. Everything external starts internal so discipline your thought patterns. Focus and visualize on it consistently, and you will be compelled and inspired to do the work and make the invisible become visible.

Motivational Drive is Fueled by your WHY

Motivation can launch us forward with a burning desire to accomplish our dreams, but how do we re-kindle that fire and passion when it begins to fade? I preached a message one time called, *"Not just Stirred but Changed."* Remember the last speaker you heard at the end of a Saturday training, a self-development seminar or church revival? Remember the energy you had when you left the meeting and how you felt like you could run through a wall?

How long did it last before you slipped back into the routine of everyday life or your level of activity come to a screeching halt? You must revive your motivational fire for the long haul so you learn to stay focused and consistent.

Connect your motivation to something you care about. Something you will not quit on! You will quit on getting a fancy car or mansion and even quit on yourself most days. Have a WHY (purpose) that drives you beyond your fears and makes you take the action necessary to live the life you desire. The inspiration that we often thrive on will soon fade back to the ease and comfort of daily routines. It doesn't require much to be ordinary or average. We often go to church or local meetings and get jacked up about what we want to accomplish, just to go home and realize the fuzzy feeling is fading quickly. Life hits you square in the face, and you are sidetracked. The reason we lose the connection with that energy (motivation) is because we haven't attached it to something we sincerely care about—something that drives us and pushes us.

People aren't born motivated, people become motivated by their own burning desire to achieve something that is important to them. People press through difficulties when they are a part of something bigger than themselves. If you can attach things to your cause/crusade/movement, you will find a new level of energy to stay motivated and driven.

Remember Your WHY. Take a moment to reflect on why you do what you do, why you desire what you desire and chase the dream that you chase. If you haven't figured out your WHY yet, do this RIGHT NOW!

When your goal is to give your very best, even the obstacles become opportunities to move forward. The mountains seem like hills. Instead of planning how little you can get by with doing, get enthusiastic and passionate about how powerful you are as the architect of your own future. Choose to feel empowered by your ability to take control and make a difference. There's everything to be gained by fully investing yourself in the work you're doing. Decide to throw yourself fully into what you're doing. Leave nothing to chance. Do yourself a big favor, and decide to go beyond just getting by. Rise above your circumstances, and experience a shift in your life that will launch you from even to overflow. From victim to victor; from just getting by to abundance and prosperity!

Most people do just enough to get by; therefore most people stay where they are. An uncommon paycheck will require an uncommon pursuit. You can make your efforts truly count for something amazing if you put forth a little more effort.

As long as you're doing the work, you might as well use the opportunity to create something meaningful. As long as you're putting in the time, you might as well get significant rewards from what you're doing. If your attitude is to just get by, you're setting yourself up for frustration and resentment. The life you desire deserves your very best efforts.

Recognize Distractions

You have probably heard the statement, "LIFE is a distraction." And the leaders who truly want to reach the top of their pay plan learn to accept and understand that "All Distractions are Equal." The difference is learning how to work through distractions and remain focused.

Building a business is a process, which takes absolute consistency. When you go a week, a month or two months without consistently working your business, it's like starting all over again. Champions are just able to confront whatever comes their way. Chances are you work with a leader who is going through things behind the scenes that would blow your mind. They realize that all distractions are equal! They choose to work through them.

Choose to work through distractions. You will successfully face any distraction and become unstoppable with that commitment!

You'll soon be saying, "Bring on the distractions!" Nothing can keep you from your ultimate goal with the right attitude. Make every day count. Make moments more valuable and meaningful. You cannot afford to waste this moment.

CHAPTER NINE

THE ENEMY!
Only Submits To Authority

"And God blessed them, and God said unto them, Be fruitful, and multiply, and replenish the earth, and subdue it: and have dominion over the fish of the sea, and over the fowl of the air, and over every living thing that moveth upon the earth." Genesis 1:28

God gave you the AUTHORITY to "subdue" earth.

Subdue means to conquer, defeat, and overcome.[vi] You were created to conquer and have dominion—to have authority on the earth!

God designed us to rule and have dominion from the beginning. We must learn to subdue mountains, systems, fears, thoughts and anything that limits us from experiencing the life we were created to live.

(89)

Few recognize their authority within the Kingdom of God. Twelve disciples shook nations and changed governments. Prophets of God brought destruction or prosperity to every atmosphere they entered based on how the people received them. God desires for you to walk in unwavering faith and start flowing in the realm of the supernatural. Be bold in your Faith to DECLARE and DECREE all of God's word with authority and unwavering faith. Watch miracles take place.

No limitations; nothing is impossible with him.

You were predestinated to live victorious. You are a wealth creator, a mountain mover, an influencer of nations, an innovator with God ideas, a trailblazer and trendsetter, and you possess the power to change history. Whatever you desire, you can have in prayer, if you BELIEVE.

So do you believe? Do you really BELIEVE? So many born again believers have relinquished their position of authority. Why would you surrender your right to access and demonstrate the power of God? You have access through the Holy Ghost to be a mountain mover. Why would you climb mountains you have been given the authority to speak to and move? Too many today have a form of Godliness, but they deny the power of God (2 Timothy 3:5).

"Now in the morning as he returned into the city, he hungered. And when he saw a fig tree in the way, he came to it, and found nothing thereon, but leaves only, and said unto it, Let no fruit grow on thee henceforward for ever. And presently the fig tree withered away. And when the disciples saw *it*, they marveled, saying, How soon is the fig tree withered away! Jesus answered and said unto them, Verily I say unto you, "If ye have faith, and doubt not, ye

shall not only do this *which is done* to the fig tree, but also if ye shall say unto this mountain, Be thou removed, and be thou cast into the sea; it shall be done." ALL THINGS, whatsoever ye shall ask in prayer, believing, ye shall receive. And when he was come into the temple, the chief priests and the elders of the people came unto him as he was teaching, and said, By what authority doest thou these things? And who gave thee this authority?" Matthew 21:18-23

"And Jesus came and spake unto them, saying, All power is given unto me in heaven and in earth." Matthew 28:18

Adam was God's representation on earth. He had dominion on earth. As the Son of Man, he was God on earth. Adam flowed in a spoken word ministry.

Everything in the Earth responded to Adam's voice. He had control over the elements. He was fully expressing the omnipotence of God. He had the power to speak to the wind, water and wildlife, and it had to obey. Yes, the first Adam fell, but the second Adam—who was Christ—redeemed us. He brought us back to that eternal relationship as sons and daughters of God. He restored all that Adam lost. That same authority and power has been restored to the saints.

To you who are spirit filled; what are you waiting on? There is no limit to God's power. Too many are living a million miles beneath their privilege. *"These signs shall follow those that believe because all things are possible to those that believe…"* (Mark 16:17). We were promised that the same unlimited supernatural power of God would be accessible to those who are Holy Ghost filled. Do you believe?

"And, behold, I send the promise of my Father upon you: but tarry ye in the city of Jerusalem, until ye be endued with power from on high." Luke 24:49

"But ye shall receive POWER, after that the Holy Ghost is come upon you." Acts 1:8

The Greek word here for power in this scripture is Dunamis. The *Analytical Lexicon of the Greek New Testament* defines with reference to Acts 1:8 as: *able to produce a strong effect power, might, strength and "as supernatural manifestations of power miracle, wonder, powerful deed."* This word is used 10 times in the Acts of the Apostles and is always in reference to God's power, miracles and signs and wonders.

We are commissioned and given a heavenly mandate to release this power, to bear witness of the resurrection power. It is time to announce who we are and WHOSE we are. Do not be satisfied with being bullied by the spiritual demonic warfare that hinders our true potential. Come out from the shadows and birth forth a revival. I know there is a group that is awakening as sons and daughters of God to a full understanding of the power they possess. Stop waiting on your pastor or even a prophetic word.

"Now unto Him that is able to do exceeding abundantly above all that we ask or think, according to the POWER that worketh IN US." Ephesians 3:20

The Kingdom of God is within you. The resurrected power of the King is within you. The omnipotent power to perform miracles abides within you. We are not powerless. This power is limited only to your faith. As much as your faith will be released, that is how much power you can have. To those who believe, you are able to conquer anything that comes before you. You have access to this power now. It has been dwelling inside of you since you accepted Jesus as your Savior! The same power that spoke the heavens and earth into existence is the same power in you now; but the key that unlocks this power is FAITH.

"And I will give unto thee the keys of the kingdom of heaven: and whatsoever thou shalt bind on earth shall be bound in heaven: and whatsoever thou shalt loose on earth shall be loosed in heaven." Matthew 16:19

"For the Kingdom of God is not just a lot of talk; it is living by God's POWER." 1 Corinthians 4:20 NLT

"...If ye have FAITH as a grain of mustard seed, ye shall say unto this mountain, Remove hence to yonder place; and it shall remove; and nothing shall be impossible unto you." Matthew 17:20

"Jesus said unto him, If thou canst BELIEVE, all things are possible to him that believeth." Mark 9:23

"Therefore I say unto you, What things soever ye "DESIRE" when ye pray, believe that ye receive them, and ye shall have them." Mark 11:24

"If ye abide in me, and my WORDS abide IN you, ye shall ask what ye will, and it shall be done unto you." John 15:7

We have quoted these scriptures all our lives, but they are useless if we do not believe. When you quote scripture without personal revelation, the result is you become an echo void of power. The Bible said it is impossible to please God without faith (Hebrews 11:6). Your faith activates the promises of God. Everything in the Kingdom is moved by Faith. Believing is the prerequisite for experiencing the supernatural. Jesus could not perform many miracles in His hometown because of unbelief. The children of Israel could not enter into the land of rest because of unbelief. They limited the Holy One of Israel because they disbelieved.

What good is quoting the infallible word of God, if you cannot believe with unwavering faith that what you are speaking will come to pass? So many people remain content with limited power, but I know the promises of *God are the same yesterday, today and forever*. This always confounds me. God is the same, yet the Bible says also different. How can someone be the same and different? God is so huge and so powerful that He's the same always, yet revealed different to us daily. When we begin to unlock the revelation that God wants to partner through us, we begin to walk in a dominion that gives us authority over every situation.

The enemy doesn't respond to formulas. He doesn't respond to rebukes. He responds to authority. God only gives authority to those who have matured in their lives to walk in that level of control. The levels of life in the Kingdom of God are as follows.

Stage One: First, we are babes. We even see this level in the life of Jesus. He was born a child (Isaiah 9:6). Children have no authority; Jesus didn't have authority when He was a child either. He was God in the flesh, but vulnerable to the outside elements of his humanity. God had to protect and hide Jesus. The same is true for us. We first come to God as babes. Useless, but anointed! We are vulnerable to enemies, circumstances and others.

Stage Two: Second, we are young adults. The next time we see Jesus in the Bible, He was a young man at the age of twelve. He was in the temple revealing that He wasn't like any other young man. He had such knowledge and understanding of God's word that Jesus kept the scholars of His day mesmerized. They were basically saying, *"Who is the young man who has such depth in the Word of God?"* (Luke 2). However, God still hadn't given Jesus authority. Some call this the manna stage. You have moved from milk to at least eating the bread of Heaven. The problem is you're vulnerable. You're full of knowledge but because you aren't fully mature, you're dangerous. You may use the power for selfish gain or feelings. So God still holds the authority to Himself.

Stage Three: The fully mature stage is the stage where God can trust us with authority. The next time we see Jesus in the Bible he was thirty years old. Think about it! We see Jesus as a baby. Then God hid Jesus and didn't reveal Him until He was twelve. After we see Jesus at twelve, God once again hid Jesus and didn't reveal Him again until He was thirty years of age. God hid Jesus for eighteen years and trained him to become fully mature. At the age of thirty, God placed the mantle of son-ship on Jesus. It is at this level where God bestows true dominion and true authority. Men would ask this question everywhere Jesus showed up. *"Who is this man that has such authority"* (Matthew 21:23)? It's at this level where the enemy now has to submit to us. We will take dominion over our world and force the enemy of poverty, sickness and lack to be subdued and controlled by us when we walk fully mature.

Kevin Mullens

CHAPTER TEN

THE COMPANY YOU KEEP!
Determines What Accompanies You

"You must constantly ask yourself these questions: Who am I around? What are they doing to me? What have they got me reading? What have they got me saying? Where do they have me going? What do they have me thinking? And most important, what do they have me becoming? Then ask yourself the big question – Is this ok?" - Jim Rohn

Your destination is often determined by the people you travel with. You eventually manifest the qualities of the company you keep.

Joseph's main secret to a life of uncommon favor, wealth and success was that the Lord was with him!

"The LORD was with Joseph, so he succeeded in everything he did as he served in the home of his Egyptian master." Genesis 39:2 NLT

We become blessed and highly favored when we are connected to men and women who understand the laws of favor and have it dripping off their lives. Keeping company with the favored will bring your entire life to another level that you could not reach on your own.

The company you keep determines what accompanies you!

You can't hang out with heroes and be a zero. Your conversations, who you associate with, who you do business with and who you stand with, will determine the outcome of your life.

"Blessed is the man who walks not in the counsel of the ungodly, Nor stands in the path of sinners, Nor sits in the seat of the scornful; but his delight is in the law of the Lord, and in His law he meditates day and night. He shall be like a tree planted by the rivers of water, that brings forth its fruit in its season, whose leaf also shall not wither; And whatever he does shall prosper." Psalm 1:1-3 (New King James Version)

"He that walketh with wise men shall be wise: but a companion of fools shall be destroyed." Proverbs 13:20

Stay in contact with people who have the virtues you desire. Pursue their wisdom. Lot was blessed because he accompanied Abraham, the blessed (Genesis 13:5). Identify people who have qualities in their life that support your desires to please God and to reach your full potential. Ask yourself; whose company am I seeking?

Wrong people birth wrong seasons; right people birth prosperous seasons. You need to remove those who are not supportive of your dreams. Silence the advice of anyone that creates chaos in your journey.

There are a lot of "Destiny Hi-Jackers" who will tell you that it is wrong to want more. I could preach right here, but I will simply suggest that the nature of almighty God within you creates the appetite for more abundance, increase and overflow. The critic will tell you that it is wrong to want more money, to want more success and to want more "things."

Quickly connect to those who add value and challenge you to step up and become MORE. To earn more you must become MORE. As the CEO of your own destiny, make sure those you allow in the boardroom of your mind are in alignment with your vision and God's word. Choose wisely those you work with and whose voice influences you.

Why is it so important to connect with the right people?

"You are the average of the five people you spend the most time with." Jim Rohn

If you are an eagle you do not belong in a barnyard roosting with the chickens. You must associate with people who are destiny conscious. We often settle because our buddies aren't driven so we have little motivation to dream bigger, do MORE and be MORE! Make sure you surround yourself with people who challenge you to become your very best; people whose very presence makes you uncomfortable with mediocrity. It is in this atmosphere that you'll elevate to higher levels and live as a reacher!

"You need partners not parasites. Partners invest in your destiny to help you succeed. Parasites extract energy in your present to sabotage your future." - Dr. Jerry Grillo

Are the people you are connected to making more withdrawals than deposits? Never compromise your destiny for company. Release people from your life that cause confusion and delay.

Everyone can't go to the next season with you. Learn when to let people go.

Separate yourself from complainers. I have always said complaining weakens faith. It was something my mom and dad wouldn't tolerate. I learned quickly to take ownership and figure things out. The children of Israel ended up taking forty years to get to the Promised Land, and it was only a five day journey. WHY? They constantly murmured—which is a word for grumbling and complaining—about God's provided way. WOW!

We definitely live in a society that wants to find every reason or excuse possible to explain their circumstances. Be quick to identify those connected to you who spend a majority of their time complaining or whining without offering resolution. It creates a negative energy that can infiltrate a group and cause distraction, confusion and destruction. Complaining is an indication that your walk with God is still attached to emotions instead of the WORD. Complaining is the act of reinforcing what you don't want and intending even more of it. Complainers will tell you their reality is causing their complaints, but it is more accurate to say, their reality is reflecting their complaints. Complainers manifest a negative life. A positive thinker will manifest a predominantly positive life. Every thought is an intention, and complainers habitually intend what they don't want. What are you intending?

"If you are in a financial rut, or looking to grow your wealth, stop complaining" - T Harv Eker

"Do everything without complaining and arguing." Philippians 2:14 NLT

"Don't complain as some of them did. The angel of death destroyed them." 1 Corinthians 10:10 (God's Word)

Separate yourself from lazy people.

"Joshua asked the Israelites, How long will you be SLACK to go in and possess the land which the Lord, the God of your fathers, has given you?" Joshua 18:3 (Amplified Bible, Classic Edition)

Do not let the enemy continue to rob you of your awesome inheritance. It's rightfully yours, but you will not inherit the abundance that flows in the Promised Land if you aren't willing to fight. Declaring and speaking your desires is only part of the process. There must be relentless ACTION.

"He becometh poor that dealeth with a SLACK hand: but the hand of the diligent maketh rich." Proverbs 10:4

"One who is SLACK in his work is brother to one who destroys." Proverbs 18:9 NIV

"Laziness moves so slow that poverty eventually overtakes it."
- Benjamin Franklin

"Be ashamed to catch yourself idle." - Benjamin Franklin

"LAZY people want much but get little, but those who work hard will prosper." Proverbs 13:4 NLT

MOVE AWAY from lazy people!

Have you heard of the phrase, "Empty vessels make the most noise?" It's a proverb that means that those with the least talent and knowledge usually speak the most and are the loudest. They love to project their negative energy in order to bring you down to their level.

We can often feel guilty or somehow think we deserve it when these empty vessels start making accusations about our new journey if we are not careful. Do not allow their emptiness to consume one minute of your time. Do not become a victim. Your focus and positive energy is so needed to manifest the life you desire, that it's necessary for you to recognize their agenda and move on. Never allow your life to be a dartboard for the naysayers of the world. Instead surround yourself with people that support your dreams and add value to your journey.

Let go of 'Destiny Hi-Jackers' who disguise themselves as friends. Surround yourself with people who support your vision and will hold you accountable. Success can be inspired through the right associations. If you want results, walk with people who get results.

The enemy wants to silence your voice, sabotage your mission, and hold your emotions as a prisoner. Decide today to prove your critics wrong by massively succeeding. You get to choose the opinions that matter to you. So choose wisely and remain in control.

Kevin Mullens

CHAPTER ELEVEN

BECOME A LIFE TIME GIVER! So You Can Be A Life Time Receiver

"I choose to rise up out of that storm and see that in moments of desperation, fear, and helplessness, each of us can be a rainbow of hope, doing what we can to extend ourselves in kindness and grace to one another. And I know for sure that there is no them – there's only us." - Oprah Winfrey

You must ultimately work to create abundance for others to live a life of abundance. What I make happen for others, God will make happen for me. Serve to create increase for others, and happiness is your reward. My wealth is in direct proportion to how many people I help (1 Corinthians 10:24).

I have 2 questions for you.

1. *Is your life encouraging others?*
2. *Does your life discourage others?*

I want to invite you into a world you may never have had the privilege of living in; a world where you become the miracle and the answer to many hurting people. Allow me to show you a world that God Himself will partner with you to fulfill. That world is what I call the giver's world. It's where you now put value and credence to your prosperity. It's where you are now blessed to be a blessing.

The life of a giver is a rich life.

If you make the time to help other people, you are rich. As soon as you give that time, you are rich. It is one of the greatest gifts you can give. If you provide financial resources to someone or a charity in need, you are instantly rich. There are many people in need, and financial resources can alleviate much pain and suffering. As soon as you give money—sow seed—you are rich.

KINDNESS IS POWER!

A random act of kindness for someone you don't know and who will never have the ability to repay you, makes you rich. Your willingness to give to strangers with no expectation of being repaid, makes you rich. If you don't believe that you can do these things, that belief makes you poor. We all have the capacity to pay it forward and make a contribution. You may have less to give than many others, but it is your willingness to give that makes you rich. It is also what will bring you true happiness, meaning and purpose. Even if you would not consider yourself wealthy by today's standards, the fact that you have the ability to give is what makes you rich. You are rich even if you only give a dollar, or an hour of your time or a kind word. When you decide to be a giver, you've decided to be rich. As a matter of fact, in God's eyes, you're already rich. Every time you interact with someone else, you have the opportunity to give that person some kind of value and form of self-worth. Imagine what you can do to advance others—whether it is a thing, a thought, a gesture or a kind word. The most powerful gifts are those that come straight from the heart. When you give more and more, you will always have more to give. Whatever leaves your hand, will never leave your life. As the joy of giving flows out from you, new richness fills your life. Give your best, and you will get even better.

"Give generously to the poor, not grudgingly, for the LORD your God will bless you in EVERYTHING you do." Deuteronomy 15:10 NLT

Wealth Principles

"Whoever is kind to the poor lends to the LORD, and He will REWARD them for what they have done." Proverbs 19:17 NIV

Give with a grateful heart…**"The generous will themselves be blessed, for they share their food with the poor."** Proverbs 22:9 NIV

"He that oppresseth the poor reproacheth his Maker: but he that honoureth him hath mercy on the poor." Proverbs 14:31

"...Inasmuch as ye have done it unto one of the least of these my brethren, ye have done it unto ME." Matthew 25:40

"When the Son of man shall come in his glory, and all the holy angels with him, then shall he sit upon the throne of his glory: And before him shall be gathered all nations: and he shall separate them one from another, as a shepherd divideth his sheep from the goats: And he shall set the sheep on his right hand, but the goats on the left. Then shall the King say unto them on his right hand, Come, ye blessed of my Father, inherit the kingdom prepared for you from the foundation of the world: For I was an hungered, and ye gave me meat: I was thirsty, and ye gave me drink: I was a stranger, and ye took me in: Naked, and ye clothed me: I was sick, and ye visited me: I was in prison, and ye came unto me. Then shall the righteous answer him, saying, Lord, when saw we thee an hungered, and fed thee? or thirsty, and gave thee drink? When saw we thee a stranger, and took thee in? or naked, and clothed thee? Or when saw we thee sick, or in prison, and came unto thee? And the King shall answer and say unto them, Verily I say unto you, Inasmuch as ye have done it unto one of the least of these my brethren, ye have done it unto me." Matthew 25:31-40

The judgment here needs no interpretation. Christ said that what you do unto the least, you do unto Him. We entertain angels unaware. Stories are told of those who have experienced such encounters where the angel was often a homeless person or a castaway. Our response is difficult sometimes because of those seeking to use their circumstances for ill-gotten gain. Many have become skilled beggars, and if we are not careful we will assume everyone is just looking for a meal ticket. That type of thinking will only add to the problem versus alleviate it. Our job is to be considerate to those less fortunate. We are blessed to be a blessing. The intent of money is not to keep it, but to give it away to create a life of significance. We are to live in a perpetual state of paying it forward, which when broken down, is really just the Golden Rule. Be mindful that the judgment of God was contingent on how we treat God, His messengers, ministry and fellow Christians. Are we capable of tending to the needs of those we do not necessarily see eye to eye with doctrinally or go to church with, as the Good Samaritan did? It is difficult, but everyone is potentially a son or daughter of God. When we love them as such, we seal our reward in eternity.

"Then shall he say also unto them on the left hand, Depart from me, ye cursed, into everlasting fire, prepared for the devil and his angels: For I was an hungered, and ye gave me no meat: I was thirsty, and ye gave me no drink: I was a stranger, and ye took me not in: naked, and ye clothed me not: sick, and in prison, and ye visited me not. Then shall they also answer him, saying, Lord, when saw we thee an hungered, or athirst, or a stranger, or naked, or sick, or in prison, and did not minister unto thee? Then shall he answer them, saying, Verily I say unto you, Inasmuch as ye did it not to one of the least of these, ye did it not to me. And these shall go away into everlasting punishment: but the righteous into life eternal." Matthew 25:41-44

With so much division and chaos surrounding us today it is apparent that our duty as ambassadors of Heaven is to show compassion (Jude 22), to love the Lord with all our heart and to love our neighbors as ourselves. The apostle Paul went on to write in Galatians 5:14 (NIV), *"For the entire law is fulfilled in keeping this one command: Love your neighbor as yourself."*

We have been commissioned to show love, as love conquers all. We are to love our enemies. I really struggle with this one sometimes, as it's so easy to love and do good to those that do good to you. Jesus went on to say, *"...Bless those that curse you, do good to them that hate you and to pray for them that despitefully mistreat you or persecute you"* (Matthew 5:45). I pray daily for God's divine love to radiate and flow through me so I can sincerely pray and give to those who do not like me. My desire is to be considerate and give to those who cannot help or promote my cause in any way.

Solomon teaches in Proverbs 25:21-22 that if your enemy is hungry, feed them or if they are thirsty, give them drink. Solomon later explains how your kindness heaps burning coals of fire upon your enemy's head. This is how you remedy hate and ultimately resolve conflict. The real conquerors are those who forgive. This is how you melt away those who choose vengeance. As the world darkens, we pay forward the hope that God has given us. If your kindness does not soften their hearts and bring about change, then judgment falls from our righteous King. It is God who will curse those who curse you. We are not to render evil for evil, but to overcome evil with GOOD! Let us aim to be merciful according to the mercy our Heavenly Father has shown unto us. When we were yet wretched sinners consumed with selfish lust, God loved us, forgave us, comforted, protected and blessed us.

God, help me to show forth love, kindness and generosity as you've shown to me unconditionally!

The world doesn't need more religion. It needs more love, and when we love one another in spite of our differences we lead people to Christ. The religious sought to stone the woman caught in adultery, but Jesus gave her a pardon. He fellowshipped with sinners, as His purpose was to save that which was lost.

You may know the Bible backwards and forwards, but do you know the Author of the Word? We can look righteous and holy, but if we fail to love, our testimony is useless. Prophet William Branham would say, *"I'd rather have a man wrong in his doctrine and right in his spirit than to have a man wrong in his spirit but right in his doctrine."* When you are right in your spirit then everything will fall into place. We must strive to be Christ-like. I have been guilty many times of almost becoming hateful or prideful in my revelation of God's Word, but what good would my revelation be if I could not help anyone see the love of God? I no longer try to lead people to a doctrine or church, but rather lead them to a merciful Father who cares for them.

I am pointing toward Calvary where the only One worthy has paid the penalty for our sins. We were all flat broke and needed someone who could pay our debt.

"For God so loved the world that he gave his only begotten Son, that whosoever believeth in him should not perish, but have everlasting life." John 3:16

"Greater love hath no man than this, that a man lay down his life for his friends. " John 15:13

Let love flow through you and brighten every corner of your world. Let love flow abundantly from you and illuminate the unique and miraculous richness in every unfolding moment. Let love live within you and spread beauty through all you do.

Let love be with all you have and all you are.

As recipients of this incredible gift, we recognize our responsibility is to spend our life giving. Our job is to reach back down and help someone else achieve the success and victory once we do! Take your experiences that have served you well and make a contribution through paying it forward without obligation. Real joy does not come from what you extract out of life. Real meaningful joy is the joy you choose to GIVE to life.

"Though I speak with the tongues of men and of angels, and have not charity, I am become as sounding brass, or a tinkling cymbal. And though I have the gift of prophecy, and understand all mysteries, and all knowledge; and though I have all faith, so that I could remove mountains, and have not charity, I am nothing. And though I bestow all my goods to feed the poor, and though I give my body to be burned, and have not charity, it profiteth me nothing. Charity suffereth long, and is kind; charity envieth not; charity vaunteth not itself, is not puffed up, Doth not behave itself unseemly, seeketh not her own, is not easily provoked, thinketh no evil; Rejoiceth not in iniquity, but rejoiceth in the truth; Beareth all things, believeth all things, hopeth all things, endureth all things. Charity never faileth...And now abideth faith, hope, charity, these three; but the greatest of these is charity." 1 Corinthians 13:1-8, 13

Let us live in such a way that our actions give charity a voice! Instead of deliberating about what needs to done; let our charitable actions roar thunderously! The key to unlocking prosperity and self-fulfillment is charity. I am not talking about just giving from your possessions but selflessly giving of yourself. This is how miracles are born. This is creating a legacy.

"Hell has forged no weapon against a person who decides to walk in love." - Dr. Jerry Grillo

Kevin Mullens

CONCLUSION

God is very progressive in the lives of His children. He is always encouraging us to reach higher, keep growing and increasing both in spiritual and natural realms. Maybe you are thinking that you have reached your goals or have possibly reached your capacity, but God has not performed and accomplished His best in your past. There is more to come. So much more!

If you are a preacher, you haven't preached your best sermon yet. If you are an author, you haven't written your best book yet. If you're an entrepreneur, you haven't built your most successful business yet. No matter what industry you are engaged in, it is time to enlarge your vision. Paul Orberson would say, *"It's time to get your hopes up."*

There is a vast and rich treasure of untapped potential within you. No matter what you have accomplished to date. Don't live on yesterday's victories and think somehow you've plateaued. God did not intend for you to only impact your local community. He said, *"You're the light of the WORLD."* He said, *"You are the salt of the EARTH."* There is so much more God has created you for. You have got more mountains to climb, bigger dreams to pursue and materialize. You are a high performance vessel fueled by the spirit of God, and your capabilities are immeasurable. I know God has been good to you, but I promise you it can be "GOODER." There is the "you" that existed before this physical "you" showed up.

"Before I formed thee in the belly I knew thee; and before thou camest forth out of the womb I sanctified thee, and I ordained thee a prophet unto the nations." Jeremiah 1:5

You have the opportunity right now to make an effort that will make a difference. It is more valuable to have some "oops" in life than continually live with "what if." Make the effort, do the work and do it well. Create real value with your time, and move ahead with no regrets. You are much more powerful, creative and effective than you give yourself credit for. You are worthy of the best in life because you are able to give your very best to each day.

Don't throw this moment away by pretending to be something you're not. The opportunities you seek in life do not come someday or tomorrow or in some vague and distant future. They are here, and they are NOW. You are limitless because you serve a God with no limitations. The opportunity of your life is NOW. Take that opportunity TODAY, while it's here, and unleash your full potential and experience the richness that is already yours.

Excuses are easy, and are completely worthless. Real, focused, consistent work can be difficult and challenging but can achieve incredible results. You fill tomorrow with regret when you waste today with excuses.

Yes, the work can be tiring, frustrating and inconvenient, yet you absolutely can get it done if you make a decision. Regret, on the other hand, is impossible to escape once you've created it. It is far better to use your time to create value rather than regret. Instead of taking the easy way out, take the truly best way forward. This hour, this day, this week, you are depositing your efforts into the lasting experiences of your life. Be sure to fill those deposits with meaningful, positive experiences rather than with painful regret.

Choose to invest yourself in the life you have dreamed about instead of wasting your time and energy on how bad your undesired circumstances are. Don't ever settle. Rather than holding back your purpose under meaningless distractions, choose to go fulfill and express that purpose with targeted actions.

Whatever things you can imagine, you can create. Though it requires effort and commitment, you are absolutely capable of making it happen. Remind yourself that this moment is not merely happening to you. It is happening through you. You can make it happen in a way that brings great richness and fulfillment to your life. You can choose to be a positive force by directing your time and energy into those things that truly matter.

Right now, you have great power to do great things. Greater is He that is within you (I John 4:4)! Greatness is your destiny. Do not neglect that desire placed within your heart. Life is not about just getting by. Do not listen to the voice of the enemy who whispers complacency and satisfaction as if that's somehow more righteous. Life is about reaching ever higher, building one achievement on top of another and creating real, meaningful value in each moment. You are destined for much more spectacular things. This is your precious and unique life, and it is absolutely worth all the trouble and effort you must go through to make it great.

Declare God's Word in your life and truly believe that it is okay to be wealthy. Slay the giants that stand in your way, and recognize you are powerful beyond measure. You are designed to live victorious. No more excuses. ONLY RESULTS! There are beautiful dreams and heartfelt desires that have been living patiently and hopefully within you. Today is the best opportunity to bring them more fully to life.

You will not waste away in a barren desert! Your time of flourishing is now! Prepare to walk fully in your destiny calling. I pray that everything and everyone that has placed limitations on you is now removed. Nothing will hinder your greatness. Barriers standing in your way of progress, advancement and prosperity are broken and removed. God's mercy is canceling the hurt of your past.

Your history is not your destiny. Mercy is rewriting your life.

Declare: I will no longer labor without getting the results I desire! My abundant harvest will no longer be hindered. I am entering my season where my cup runs over.

You must embrace the life God imagined or foresaw. Your dissatisfaction is the revelation that you are MORE because He is MORE!

i Marianne Williamson

ii https://www.merriam-webster.com/dictionary/surplus

iii http://www.bloodyelbow.com/2015/4/5/8343909/conor-mcgregor-dethrone-jose-aldo-ufc-189

iv http://www.menprovement.com/the-power-of-belief-2/

v http://www.amazingwomeninhistory.com/wilma-rudolph-olympic-gold-medalist-civil-right-pioneer/

vi https://www.merriam-webster.com/dictionary/subdue